Praise for *You Are Creative*

"In racing, people often talk about instinct or talent, but what they don't see is the process behind it. Preparation, analysis, learning from mistakes, and then executing when the moment comes—those steps are what separate a good performance from a winning one.

Reading Emilio DiIorio's exploration of the creative process felt familiar. His framework—from preparation and incubation to insight and implementation—mirrors what happens in every field where performance matters.

Creativity isn't just for artists. It's the ability to think clearly, adapt, and bring ideas into reality under real-world conditions.

You Are Creative is for people who want to perform better, solve problems more effectively, and stay competitive."

—Mario Andretti, World Champion Race Car Driver

"*You Are Creative* is a must-read for anyone seeking an edge in an era where knowledge is increasingly commoditized by AI. Dr. Emilio DiIorio dismantles the myth that creativity is innate, offering actionable steps to foster innovation. Drawing on anecdotes from his own distinguished career and insights from across industries, the book serves as a practical road map for anyone ready to cultivate meaningful breakthroughs."

—Jimmy Chang, Chief Investment Officer,
Rockefeller Global Family Office

"*You Are Creative* is a refreshing and much-needed corrective to the mythology that surrounds creativity. Rather than mystifying the process, he illuminates it—step by step—with clarity, humility, and insight. What stands out most is how transferable his approach is: Whether in a studio, a laboratory, or a classroom, his five-stage framework offers a reliable path forward that is informed by research and practice. This is an inspiring yet grounded guide for anyone ready to move from idea to action with intention."

—Dr. William B. Crow, Professor, Lehigh University, and former Educator-in-Charge of Teaching and Learning, Metropolitan Museum of Art

"In *You Are Creative*, Emilio DiIorio deconstructs the premise that creativity belongs only to artists and visionaries, revealing it instead as a disciplined, acquirable process inherent to the human experience. Drawing from his remarkable journey through engineering, medicine, entrepreneurship, and the arts, DiIorio offers a compelling five-stage framework that is both intellectually rigorous and deeply human. This book is at once practical and inspiring, serving as a guide for anyone who wants to solve meaningful problems, unlock original ideas, and live more fully. A powerful reminder that creativity is not a gift for the few, but a calling for us all."

—Robert A. Flowers, II, PhD, Herbert J. and Ann L. Siegel
Dean, College of Arts & Sciences, Lehigh University

"In my work growing the Lehigh Valley business community, I've seen how purpose-driven leadership transforms organizations and lives. Dr. Emilio DiIorio is a rare kind of leader. From keeping first-class athletes performing at the highest level to building an incredible regional health network from the ground up, Emilio understands what it means to build something that matters.

His book, *You Are Creative,* lays out a clear, experience-based framework for aligning your talents with service—and creating impact that extends well beyond yourself. I'm all in on every page of this book."

—Tony Iannelli, President and CEO, Greater Lehigh Valley Chamber of Commerce, the sixth-largest Chamber in the US

"Over the course of my career—as a fine artist, industrial designer, and automotive designer—I've seen creativity expressed in many forms. What they all share is process. Great ideas develop through preparation, reflection, iteration, and, ultimately, the discipline to make something real.

You Are Creative brings clarity and humanity to the creative process. His five-part framework—preparation, incubation, insight, evaluation, and implementation—offers a road map for how creativity can be practiced. The discipline, self-motivation, and, above all, the persistence to make the incredible happen.

If you are ready to move from ideas to meaningful creation, this book is your guide."

—Peter Maier, Fine Artist and former Senior Exterior Automobile Designer, Cadillac, Pontiac, and Chevrolet Motor Divisions, General Motors Corporation

YOU ARE CREATIVE

YOU ARE CREATIVE

A Five-Stage Process to Unlock Ideas, Solve Problems, and Find Possibility Everywhere

EMILIO DIIORIO

MATT HOLT

Matt Holt Books
An Imprint of BenBella Books, Inc.
Dallas, TX

Matt Holt is an imprint of BenBella Books, Inc.
BenBella Books, Inc.
8080 N. Central Expressway
Suite 1700
Dallas, TX 75206
benbellabooks.com
Send feedback to feedback@benbellabooks.com

Matt Holt and *BenBella* are federally registered trademarks.

Printed in the United States of America
10 9 8 7 6 5 4 3 2 1

Library of Congress Control Number: 2026011157
ISBN 9798902680130 (hardcover)
ISBN 9798902680147 (electronic)

Editing by Katie Dickman
Copyediting by Jennifer Brett Greenstein
Proofreading by Lisa Story and Jenny Bridges
Text design and composition by PerfecType, Nashville, TN
Cover design by Jason Arias
Printed by Lake Book Manufacturing

To my wife, Amanda, for her love, encouragement, and support

and

to my teachers in systems engineering, surgery, and sculpture,

who taught me what it means to be creative

CONTENTS

Part 3: Beyond the Studio

INTRODUCTION: YES, YOU ARE CREATIVE

Something drew you to this book. Perhaps, deep down, you have the sense that there is more to you than your current job title or role in life. Perhaps you have never even thought of yourself as "creative." I want to assure you that you most definitely are creative—no matter what you do or who your title says you are. As an engineer, surgeon, entrepreneur, and artist, I can safely say that most people entirely misunderstand the true nature of creativity—what it entails, how it works, and why it is so important. I have found creativity to be vital to every aspect of the varied careers I've had and, especially, to my life. The purpose of this book is to show you that anyone can be creative and that a universal framework for creativity exists. Creativity is:

- A scientific process.
- Not just for artists. It's for individuals of all backgrounds, professions, and walks of life. Creativity is for everyone.
- A behavior and mindset, not an identity.

- Something that is learned. Creativity isn't something a select few are "born with"—rather, it's a skill and a process that can be taught, cultivated, and practiced if you know the processes and how creativity works.
- Made up of love, passion, and curiosity, the essential ingredients to being fully human and living the creative life. What does it mean to be fully human? In my mind, being fully human simply means fulfilling our ultimate purpose. And without a doubt, that purpose is to create. We are all creators of our own lives, and collectively we create the world. When we aren't creating, we are dying. To be fully human means to be creative. And we are all creative.

My intention in this book is to unravel the myths and commonly held misconceptions about what it means to live and work creatively. This is a book about the science and the art of creativity: namely, the skills and processes required to be creative that are backed by neuroscience, biology, and behavioral psychology, as well as by the habits, practices, and wisdom of the creative greats who have come before us.

Why Creativity Is Essential in Today's World

I started my journey through the creative life during the late sixties and early seventies, when the United States was facing a revolution of thought. I was in my early teens and twenties and kids my age didn't want to be drafted. They didn't want to follow the paths their parents set for them. Most young men didn't want to join the military as their fathers did before them in World War II. Most young women didn't want to become housewives and mothers; rather, they wanted careers outside the home. But in colleges we were being prepared for a world that valued our humanity less than our ability to produce and consume. Today, we are facing a different kind of revolution, but a revolution all the same. It was born out of the COVID-19 pandemic, which sparked an increase in work-from-home and hybrid office jobs and the mass exodus from standard office work environments known as the Great Resignation. This exodus occurred largely because employees realized that their working conditions were poor, their quality of life was unsatisfactory, and their wages were low. Together these two crises have brought to light that many people are deeply dissatisfied with their work and feel stuck in jobs that lack meaning and purpose. In our hyperconnected world, we spend an increasing amount of time on our computers and our phones, and some of us can do our work almost anywhere. And regardless of where we work, our fully wired world can be overwhelming. The workplace is changing, and the digital world is here to stay. Mastering the science of creativity will help us all thrive in this digital world.

We also know that in a world that is becoming more dependent on artificial intelligence, employers increasingly look for and reward employees who think creatively and innovate. Our best protection against AI will be to fire up our creativity—something technology cannot do. As Will Gompertz, author of *Think Like an Artist*, put it, "We live in a world full of urgent problems: climate change, terrorism, and poverty, to name but three. We won't resolve them with brawn; they are obstacles we can only overcome by using our brains—when we are thinking like artists and not behaving like animals."[1]

If we're not behaving like animals, we're going to need to adopt certain behaviors and mindsets—hard work, self-awareness, discipline, and the exercise of creative patterns in a consistent manner—to do so.

---

1. Will Gompertz, *Think Like an Artist . . . and Lead a More Creative, Productive Life* (Penguin Press, 2015), 45.

Where I Create: Atelier Lucca

As an artist, I realize that whether it be painting or sculpture, my creativity is emotional and spontaneous. It is something I am fortunate to have. Something that at times can be almost spiritual. The members of my art teams are of similar types. The environment we have created at Atelier Lucca, my current studio in Bethlehem, Pennsylvania, where I create my sculptures and paintings, helps us sharpen our skills and collect our creative ideas. Here we have an eighteen-thousand-square-foot building. It displays and stores my extensive collection, and we have additional sculpture studio space, a photography suite, space for a writer's workshop, and administrative offices. We also have surrounding botanical gardens that spread throughout the eleven-acre campus. The gardens of Atelier Lucca were designed and are managed by a horticultural team led by Amanda DiIorio and her head gardener. These gardens, parts of which are modeled after Monet's estate at Giverny, are important influences on the campus art production. The arts we practice consist of sculpture, painting, horticulture, and creative writing.

We also employ several off-site facilities to enhance our technology and editing capabilities: CNC marble milling in Brooklyn, New York; digital scanning of sculpture by a company in Hamilton, New Jersey; a bronze and steel foundry in Lancaster, Pennsylvania; and consultant writers and editors in Cincinnati, Ohio. In total, the people that make up the cross-field teams include sculptors, painters, writing consultants, horticulturists, landscape architects, artisan woodworkers, technologists, photographers, and administrators. We are all creative, though some of us wouldn't readily call ourselves "artists."

We are located approximately ninety miles west of Manhattan and also have smaller ancillary sites in Tribeca (Manhattan) and the Pocono Mountains. The Poconos are also the site of our three-hundred-acre regenerative organic farm (Teaberry Fields & Forest), containing forests, pastures, and gardens, as well as some pampered chickens, sheep, pigs, cattle, and Gabriel (a Belgian horse).

We are a group of like-minded creative individuals who believe truth and nature to be one. We are people who ask, Is it good? Is it beautiful? Is it interesting?

My art and studio are made infinitely better by the team and systems I have in place. And I learned how to build teams and systems in the very real world of work. While I use all five stages of the creative process (discussed later in this book) in the creation of my art, I realize it's easy for people to say, "Well, that's very good for you, Emilio, you're a sculptor, but what about me? I work in [insert profession here]." It is then that I say, "I also worked in the healthcare and engineering fields, and I even manage my studio. And these stages work for me as well." My approach to creativity here was a deliberate mental process of acquiring knowledge and understanding. Creativity, and sometimes innovation, came from hard work in a particular area of healthcare. I repeated trials and made tweaks until something worked better. Just as I rely on my team in my sculpture studio, when I was developing my company, HCDS, I relied on clinical and administrative teams collaborating regularly and learning from one another. And just as I relied on all my past experience and studies in drawing, art, and sculpture when forming my art studio, I relied on deliberate mental creativity and knowledge in order to combine existing information in new and innovative ways in healthcare. At HCDS this went on for over thirty years.

The Difference Between Creative and Artistic

Many people go through life believing that since they are not artistic, they are not creative. This is because they believe creativity and artistry are one and the same—they are not!

The creative person uses a mental process to develop ideas to solve a problem (this process is the subject of this book). An artistic person uses a physical process to create tangible works of art (painting, sculpture, composition, music, poetry, dance, architecture). *While only some of us have innate artistic talent, all of us can be creative.* The creative artist is probably a better artist, but you do not have to be an artist to be creative. Creativity is available to all of us. And it can be learned.

Graham Wallas and the Creative Process

In part 2 of this book, I present and discuss a five-stage creative process that grows out of a creativity process developed by social psychologist Graham Wallas, which he wrote about in his book *The Art of Thought*, originally published in 1926. Wallas, who cofounded the London School of Economics, outlines four stages of the creative process, based on his own observations and the accounts of other famous inventors. I first read Wallas's book years ago, and it has remained the foundation of my thoughts on creativity. Although variations of the creative process have been developed by notable academics such as Mihaly Csikszentmihalyi, Keith Sawyer, and many others, Wallas's original four-stage framework remains most helpful for me. The method that I will present here builds on Wallas's framework.

The five stages of the creative process we will cover in the chapters of this book are:

1. Preparation: This is the research and development stage.
2. Incubation: In this stage your subconscious does the heavy lifting while you relax and let go so meaningful connection can begin to take place.
3. Insight: This stage is when you start to produce a large volume of ideas and develop various solutions using a number of thinking methodologies.

4. Evaluation: In this stage you combine your best ideas and choose the optimal one to execute.
5. Implementation: This stage is where all the previous stages come to fruition and you begin to see the "product" or result of the process.

There is no need to commit these to memory right now. We will discuss all these stages in depth in part 2.

The Purpose of This Book

The purpose of this book is to show that regardless of your personality, innate tendencies and talents, or occupation, you can indeed become creative by simply following the stages I outline. And being creative is something we can all do. Creativity has three components:

- The person: You don't have to be a "creative personality type" to create. In fact, the act of creating makes you creative. The more creative you are, the more fully human you become.
- The creative process: Creativity requires a particular process; it's a way of thinking, behaving, and then executing steps in a particular order to come up with new ideas.
- The product: The product of creativity is what results when a person enacts the creative process.

My wife, Amanda, serves as a real-life example of these three components in action. Amanda (person) is designing and building a water feature for one of our gardens. In the initial stages, she researched garden ponds and plants (process—preparation and incubation). Our mailbox received an onslaught of design and how-to books for developing whispering water sounds. There will be many stages in the process for her to go through until she has achieved her final desired outcome (product).

What to Expect in This Book

The first part of this book introduces several concepts that are foundational to creativity. You will learn about the relationship between creativity and living a "fully human" life and the difference between big "C" Creativity and small "c" creativity. I explore in depth what it really means to create, and my goal is that by the time you finish this section, you'll be convinced that you, too, are a creative person.

In the second part, we will take a deep dive into the creative process. You will learn all about preparation, incubation, insight, evaluation, and then implementation, as well as the "Jobs to Be Done" and "mindset" associated with each stage. Along the way, I'll dispel one or more creativity myths that may be holding you back.

At the end of each chapter in part 2, I will show you how creativity applies in unexpected environments by presenting my own creative process in developing my healthcare company as a case study of the process in action. These case studies are intended especially for those of you who don't necessarily identify as "creative" but see yourself as an entrepreneur or someone who solves problems daily in a business setting.

Throughout the book, I draw on my personal and professional journey—from a child of immigrants growing up in New York City; to a student of engineering, then anatomy, then medicine; to a physician and the founder of a healthcare company; to my current career as a sculptor, artist, and writer. I have lived many lives—and have had the privilege of experiencing a wide array of careers. Today I enjoy the freedom that comes from a lifetime of hard work and dedication to my craft—I can travel, work, and live in a way I could not have imagined as a young person cooking his dinner over a hot plate in a cold one-room apartment. My intention in sharing my wide range of life experiences—from mortgaging my home to fund my healthcare company to working around the clock and even napping in my car—is to demonstrate that wherever you are today, you can live a creative life, regardless of your income or lifestyle. I'd also like to remind you that contrary to popular myth, being creative can improve your earning potential.

My hope is that as you undertake the journey in this book, you will come to see that every aspect of your life can be a creative endeavor. When you commit to living your life creatively, you will find the purpose, meaning, and beauty that exist all around you. By harnessing the science of creativity, you can become fully human, and you, too, will realize that you are creative.

PART 1

The Elements of Creativity: Person, Process, and Product

CHAPTER 1

Becoming Fully Human

I try to visit Europe, especially Italy, as much as possible to find creative inspiration as well as to escape from routine and shake off the dust from my home studio. When in Florence, I always find time to pay homage to a sculptor and painter who has inspired me and whom I consider to be one of the most significant sculptors of the twentieth century, Marino Marini. I first stumbled upon his work many years ago, when I was in the middle of Middelheim Park in Antwerp. Since then, I have visited the Marino Marini Museum in Florence many times over the years and I always come away with innovative ideas.

Marini was a man from my father's generation; both were born in the first decade of the twentieth century. In certain ways, I feel connected to Marini as a son does to his father. Since my own father wasn't an artist, I consider Marini a surrogate father of sorts. He has shown me the path forward as an artist as a father might show his son his vision for the world. Though I never met Marini, I feel his guidance in my art as a son feels his father's presence long after he is gone. Marini had his first solo exhibition in New York in 1950, fifteen years before I attended college there. His teacher, Arturo Martini, another contemporary Italian sculptor, believed, as Marini did, in using the past to build a future. They both shared a deep reverence for the past, studied it, learned from it, and then transformed it and used it in their art form. They honored their Italian history of sculpture and built from it. They were the first modern Italian sculptors to use the plastic form to create sculpture with intersecting volumes reminiscent of Etruscan art. Like Marino Marini, I take our shared Etruscan ancestry seriously. The Etruscans inhabited a part of central Italy that stretched roughly from the Arno to the Tiber and that included the surrounding areas of Rome and Florence. Marini's people were from Florence (Pistoia) and mine are from Rome (and its surroundings). In this area, the Etruscans lived and formed the bedrock of Italian culture around 900 BC.[1] It was the dominant culture for seven hundred to eight hundred years before being wiped out by the Romans. But before that took place, the Etruscans taught the Romans a significant amount about art and engineering. Many of the aqueducts and bridges that people look at as marvels of Roman engineering were actually Etruscan inventions. Their tomb frescoes are a statement to their use of form and color in painting. The bronze artwork they left behind is proof of their skills in sculpture.

Marini then went on to attend art school in Florence. He worked with the female form at first and then later developed a horse and rider series of sculptures. He didn't limit himself. He was always stretching himself further. One of his objectives was the simplification of form, but ultimately he was trying to create a fusion of forms; it is

---

1. I prefer to use "BC" and "AD" and will do so throughout this book.

the combination of forms that makes a thing beautiful. He was someone who knew firsthand about pulling from the past to create a more beautiful future. He was a child during World War I, and when his studio was bombed out during World War II, he was forced to move to Switzerland. Throughout all his hardships, he continued to produce art because he said it gave him hope. He was a man dedicated to finding the joy and hope in life—even amid decay and suffering.

And even though he was an Italian from Florence, he knew that the Italians were only partly responsible for the Renaissance. He recognized that a Renaissance also took place in northern Europe—in towns like Bruges, Antwerp, and Ghent—that in some ways, especially in painting, superseded the Renaissance of Florence. Marini spent time traveling in northern Europe, something I did as well.

A Fully Human Life

I don't admire Marini solely for his abilities as a sculptor. His life embodied creativity: he lived fully, experiencing it all. He wasn't someone who settled for the status quo. He was insatiably curious, pursued his passions, and honed his skills. He not only mastered his craft but also lived his everyday life in a way that honored and celebrated love, beauty, and humanity. Furthermore, Marini was someone who was constantly pushing the boundaries of what he knew. As such, he pursued experiences beyond his areas of expertise in order to better understand the human condition.

Like Marini, I have made the quest to broaden my horizons a hallmark of my life. I am constantly seeking to expand my worldview. To be fully human requires creativity, intellect, relationships with others, morality, and a sense that there is something so much bigger than us—or what some call "spirituality." Being fully human is about having what Marini sought when he created works like the goddess of fertility,

Pomona: the ability to show hope amid the darkness, birth amid death. To be fully human means having the spaciousness to examine one's own life and one's place in it. Sometimes in life, you must be willing to walk away from something that is no longer serving you or inspiring you. You must be willing to walk away from all that you know in order to broaden your horizons and make room for yourself to become who you were meant to be.

As I look back on my life, there is no question in my mind that every time I had the opportunity to broaden my horizons and become more fully human, I took it. Whether it was leaving my MBA program and job on Wall Street to travel to Europe or deciding to become a physician and then leaving that behind to start my own healthcare system. Or most recently, leaving healthcare to sculpt. But what force helped me choose to walk away each time? It wasn't simply passion driving my decision. There was also a desire for personal growth, fulfillment, and ambition.

As humans, we all have this desire, and it's admirable. We shouldn't shy away from it. In some ways, our longing is our calling. We all have different areas of interests and different capabilities. I firmly believe that as humans, we are by nature multidimensional. We contain too much to be limited in this life by one career, one talent, one skill set. If at work or in your personal life you're no longer feeling the old spark, that's a sign to pursue a new challenge, a new opportunity. It's a sign you're ready to broaden your horizons. You were meant to be fully human, you were meant to expand your capabilities, and you were meant to help others along the way. Though Marini died before I had a chance to meet him, his life served as a model of how I wanted to live my own. His "mentorship" in a way inspired me to inspire others. He wasn't given much recognition in his time, in the sense that he was not a household name like Pablo Picasso or Andy Warhol. But he was represented by galleries in New York, London, and Zurich. He was part of a show at MoMA in 1950. He was someone who took his art (and life) seriously, and I will forever be indebted to him. He was someone whom I wanted to emulate, though in truth, it was difficult for me to do so in the beginning of my life.

My Story: From Artisans and Farmers to Astronauts, Economists, and Doctors

Born to immigrant Italian parents, I grew up in New York. As kids, my siblings and I were expected to work, go to college (and pay for it), and get well-paying jobs to support ourselves afterward. From a young age, I felt pulled toward the arts. But I questioned whether I could make a living at it. My mother had come from a long line of Italian artisans. Her father restored furniture that was found in villas in Rome, which contained paintings of Roman scenes or villas on the panels. After Mussolini and the Fascists took over Italy, my grandfather emigrated with his wife and children (including my mother) to America and soon opened and ran a successful furniture restoration business. An artist in his own right, my grandfather wasn't rich, but he was able to build a home and raise his sons to take over the business. He was someone who was able to make a living as an artist. My own father (an Italian immigrant as well) didn't think art was a worthwhile pursuit.

Though my grandfather and uncles had been artisans and fine craftsmen, I was not exposed to much art in our home, other than some hand-carved furniture and charcoal drawings done by an uncle and the Puccini opera recordings that my mother loved. I took up drawing and enjoyed it; from a young age, I was drawn to color. My father had come from a long line of farmers. He was a hard worker and expected the same from his children. I had an uncle who was an engineer. I had seen his success and I thought engineering would be a good fit for me. In high schools at the time, there was a huge push for what we now call STEM. We were in competition with Russia to put a man on the moon, and every kid in America wanted to be a part of it, myself included. I kept at my drawing even when I was studying engineering at NYU. When most of my peers were starting to dabble in drugs and participate in protests, I was studying and, whenever I could, visiting various exhibits and galleries.

When I was a teenager in the sixties, a revolution raged outside the windows of my classrooms in the form of civil rights and Vietnam War protests; beyond the campus gates, several revolutions were also occurring in the art world in New York City. The art revolution actually started in the forties with the abstract expressionism movement, spearheaded by Jackson Pollock. But by the time I was in college, art had transformed into minimalism, made famous by Frank Stella and Donald Judd. I was somewhat aware of these movements because they were happening right in my backyard. Pop art was on the rise thanks to Andy Warhol, who was also making a splash at the time because he was a genius at marketing himself. It would have been impossible for anyone living in New York not to know who he was or what he was up to. Finally, there was a conceptual art movement happening, where the emphasis was less on the aesthetic or technical aspects of the art and more on the idea behind the piece itself. Marcel Duchamp's urinal, for example, is a piece that defined the conceptual art movement at the time.

Fortunately for me, New York City catered to its students and made sure art was accessible to them by providing discounted student admission at art museums. Back then, the city also gave students special tokens to ride the subway, and students could enjoy Broadway shows at a discount too. I was able to escape to museums like the Metropolitan, the Guggenheim, and MoMA. It was at the Metropolitan that I first taught myself about art—starting with the Greeks and the Romans. But not far from the Greek and Roman exhibits was the Egyptian collection. And beside it was a small gallery dedicated to the Etruscans. It was here that I became fascinated with and began to study Etruscan art. (It wasn't until many years later, however, that I would stumble upon Marini's work.)

Heading out of class one day at NYU, I watched as buildings burned and busloads of police, armed with shields and batons, spilled out onto campus and began to beat students protesting the war in Vietnam. It was all so surreal. I couldn't afford to be dragged to a police station for protesting anything; I knew my father wasn't going to bail me out. I kept my head down and stayed far from the fray. I did the best I could to excel in engineering school, knowing how lucky I was just to be there. And I didn't feel lucky just because I was the child of immigrants. I felt lucky because I was fully aware that, while I was studying and others were protesting, many of my peers were boarding a different type of bus—one that would take them to Parris Island on their way to die in Vietnam. I was one of the lucky ones. I received a college deferment. And by the time I graduated, I was recruited by Grumman Aerospace (later Northrop Grumman), and because I had a security clearance, I was once again given a pass.

At that time, Grumman Aerospace was busy making the lunar module that would eventually take Neil Armstrong, Buzz Aldrin, and Michael Collins to the moon. Granted, I was just a junior engineer, but all of us at Grumman celebrated when the astronauts landed successfully. Eventually, all the astronauts, including Neil Armstrong, made a special visit to Grumman and thanked us for our work. Shaking Neil Armstrong's hand was one of the great thrills of my life. It affected me in ways I still can't fully articulate. After meeting him, all I knew was that I wanted to continue my education, that there was so much more I wanted to do. We, as humans, had used our creativity and superior minds and, defying all limitations, had shot for and actually landed on the moon. What more could we do?

Around that same time, a German senior economist from Berlin, Bernard Schmitz, who was consulting for Grumman, met with me and said, "You could do graduate work in economics and finance and combine it with your engineering studies." He was brilliant, and I admired him, so I decided to go for it. I had been searching for more, and though I wasn't sure if this was it, I was willing to try it. I didn't have a plan. And since Grumman would be paying for me to attend the NYU Stern School of Business (located then on Wall Street), I would have been crazy to pass it up.

And yet, even with all this education, and all the money I was making, I wasn't happy. That is to say, I was grateful, but I wasn't happy. I knew I wasn't answering my calling. I knew there was something more. It came to me while in my third year at Grumman and while studying at Stern. I had been taking evening classes, and I stepped out on Wall Street to take a walk. It was about nine or ten at night, and the usually bustling financial district was eerily empty. I looked down the street and just knew I needed to broaden my horizons. This wasn't for me. It wasn't that I didn't enjoy the graduate courses and the Grumman experience. I had everything I wanted—a good salary, opportunities for more—but there was something intangible and ineffable I hadn't attained. I didn't have the words for it, but I knew the life I was living wasn't the one for me. I also knew there was a life out there for which I was better suited. It didn't hit me like a thunderbolt. The thought simply appeared, and so I pursued it.

It was also at Grumman that I met some engineers who had studied and lived in Europe. Discussions with them opened up new possibilities for me. I looked at several schools in northern Europe and decided to study at Ghent University in Belgium. The question was, What should I study? Art? Science? At the time, I wasn't sure. I needed to figure it out. Just as Leonardo da Vinci studied anatomy as the bridge between art and science, I decided I would start with anatomy too. The school was known for not only its strong artistic reputation but also its excellent anatomy department. In many ways, my move to Europe and my studies in Ghent were my first foray into what would become the creative process that I will break down in this book. Leonardo had used extensive cadaveric dissections to understand the human anatomy, and I decided to spend an entire year at Ghent dissecting a cadaver, while documenting my progress with drawings of the bones, muscles, tendons, and joints. While drawing, I found a new purpose and a new domain of study: orthopedic surgery.

At this point I moved to Antwerp, a neighboring city steeped in both art and medicine, and began medical school. I also found time to walk up the street from my medical school and visit the house and studio of Peter Paul Rubens.

Draw, Emilio, Draw!

It wasn't such a stretch to go from engineering to anatomy and then on to orthopedic surgery. I had begun studying anatomy as an undergraduate at NYU, as part of a course I took called Human Factors Engineering. The course focused on applying human anatomy and physiology to the design of machines and jobs. It also featured designing devices and systems to make work more efficient, effective, and safe, and in order to do this, I had to understand the muscular and skeletal construction of the human body. At the time, I was surrounded by artists and there were numerous opportunities throughout the city to attend drawing classes and draw live models. For a small fee, I was able to bring my charcoals and papers and draw for an hour or two. I continued this practice in Europe, and it's an exercise that I continue to this day. The main reason I do so is that life drawing, or drawing from the model, forces the artist to focus, to look closely, and to figure out proportions. It also allows the artist to capture the movement of the body, to seize the balance between proportion, and to capture the tensions that the figure demonstrates in different positions.

I used this same understanding of anatomy as I started to draw from the model and, at the time, chose figurative art over abstract. Instead of doing what was expected of me this time around, I let my curiosity lead me. Again, I didn't have a plan, just a seed of interest that I cultivated. And at the time, it seemed like the right thing to do.

While studying at Ghent, I met a professor of anatomy, Julien "Jan" Fautrez, who taught me how to "draw and talk." He told stories as he drew and he lectured us on how the heart and the blood vessels worked together. He'd start with the embryo, describe how it developed, and go from there. When he taught anatomy, he would have us look at a picture, memorize it, draw it from memory, and then tell the story of what was happening as we drew it. Examination time with Professor Fautrez was a time to tell an intricate story with words, pictures, and colors. There were no multiple-choice questions to hide behind, but rather creative answers that showed whether or not you truly understood the topic. Then I would draw whatever he asked us to—the musculature around the pelvis and the vessels that run through it, for example. And then I would have to tell him a story about it while I drew it. As I did so, he'd say to me, "Tell me, Emilio, why did you do it that way? Why do you suppose the vessel decided to travel along that side of the muscle instead of the back of the muscle?" I'd then go on to explain the embryology, that while the muscle was developing, it only had so much room for a vessel, so the vessel had to move to the front.

Julien Fautrez was a teacher who animated human anatomy and told its story through drawing. These are lessons that I have continued to use as both a surgeon and an artist.

In the process of learning anatomy and how to "draw and talk," I was learning not only how the human body works but also how creativity works. I was learning how the creative mind, like a blood vessel, will work around obstacles to create something new and life-sustaining. I was hooked.

Process Versus Identity

I have always been someone pulled by a creative calling and have used creativity in all areas of my life—as an engineer, economist, medical student, surgeon, entrepreneur, and sculptor. Creativity is not for artists alone. As Twyla Tharp, the great choreographer and author of the book *The Creative Habit*, says, "Creativity is not just for artists. It's for businesspeople looking for a new way to close a sale; it's for engineers trying to solve a problem; it's for parents who want their children to see the world in more than one way."[2]

Yes, creativity is for *everyone*.

When I was making my way through New York at the height of the sixties, I didn't play the part of an "artist." I didn't do the drug scene. I didn't dress the part. I was floating under the radar as an engineering student. And like many others out there, I didn't think I could fully step into this creative identity. There are probably a lot of you reading this who, deep down, know you're creative, who know that you have creative instincts or use creativity every day in your career (whether you're a plumber, entrepreneur, computer programmer, accountant, marketer, lawyer, mother, gardener, or any number of other things). But you don't feel like you can say you're "Creative" with a capital "C," because your job title or personality doesn't seem to align with the definition of a creative as we commonly know it—that is, an "artist."

But I am here to say with some assurance that, after the life I have lived and the various careers I have held, the creative life came from a

---

2. Twyla Tharp, *The Creative Habit: Learn It and Use It for Life* (Simon & Schuster, 2003), 7.

longing deep within me that I kept pursuing out of curiosity and out of interest. It's a process—not a personality or an identity. And it's not simply for those of us who "identify as artists." The creative process is something everyone can learn to embrace. It's also something that will not only help you in any career you may find yourself in, but also help you live a more complete and fulfilled life.

Your Own Moon Landing

Something inside you drew you to this book—maybe you, too, feel a calling, or maybe you're curious, or maybe you just know there is so much more you're capable of doing. You know there is a proverbial moon out there to land on, but you just don't have a plan for how to get there. Or, perhaps, like I was when I was ready to leave New York, you feel trapped in your current life and career, and you must liberate yourself to survive and thrive.

If I had stayed and worked on Wall Street, I could have earned a high salary right out of school. I knew leaving my job on Wall Street to pursue my creativity meant an unpredictable income. Looking back, however, I can say that the creative path has afforded me the opportunity to live a life where I can be fully myself, fully human. It wasn't always easy, and it came with great sacrifice at first, but it hardly registered as such. I was happy and I knew, like Cicero said all those years ago, "If you have a garden and a library, you have everything you need."

The thing is, I didn't become a "creative" by following the path one might imagine. My art "studio" for the next four decades was an operating room and healthcare company I founded. Nevertheless, I was living a wholly creative existence, one of my own design. I would spend the next five decades living creatively and studying the practice of creativity as I searched for answers to the following questions: What makes a person creative? And can anyone learn to be creative?

This inquiry ultimately led me to create a framework and process that anyone can use to engineer creativity and that I will share with you in the chapters that follow.

Jump-Start Your Creativity

If you don't already, make a practice of reading with a pen and a notebook or journal on hand. As you read this book, take notes as ideas come to you and write them there. At the end of each chapter, I will list questions for you to ponder and respond to in your journal. For all the "Jump-Start Your Creativity" sections, be sure to take a moment and jot down your thoughts in your journal. If you're feeling especially inspired, draw, sketch, and make the journal your own—as ideas come to you.

I had Marino Marini as an early inspiration and guide as to how I wanted to harness creativity to live more fully. In my view, he embraced his passions, was curious, and honed his skills. He mastered not only his craft but also his life through the way he celebrated and honored love, beauty, and humanity. He was constantly using the past to create a better future, all while trying to deeply understand the human condition.

- Who is your Marino Marini? Whose life do you feel inspired by? What about this person's life appeals to you?
- What does it mean to you to become more fully human?
- What do you do that you feel is creative—even if outsiders don't seem to think so or understand? What about this activity makes you feel alive?

CHAPTER 2

Defining the Creative Person

What makes a person creative? Is creativity something we all have within us? Or is it the domain of famous artists and Nobel Prize winners?

The answer is yes to both of these questions. There are two types of creativity. The first, everyday creativity, is accessible to all of us. This type of creativity can be nurtured and enhanced and is the main topic of this book. The second type, extraordinary creativity, resides with the great geniuses. While understanding these geniuses is not the main objective of this book, the stories of these special minds can give us great insight into the creative process. For the remainder of this book, I will refer to extraordinary creativity as big "C" Creativity, and I will refer to everyday creativity as small "c" creativity.

The great thinker and writer Mihaly Csikszentmihalyi described big "C" Creativity as a system. According to Csikszentmihalyi, a big

"C" Creative works within a "domain" or a culture of symbolic rules, then works in a "field," as in a field of experts, and finally, as an individual, brings a new idea or "thing" (invention, process, product) that changes outcomes. Now, this domain can be anything—not just the "art" world. Big "C" Creativity can exist in all domains, including banking, technology, business, publishing, sports, and medicine, to name just a few.

What It Means to Be a Big "C" Creative

To illustrate what it means to be a big "C" Creative, let's go back to the spring of 1962 in a suburb of Tokyo, Japan. A seventeen-year-old boy was playing an intense pickup game of basketball. While struggling under the board for a rebound, he twisted his knee and fell to the ground. He was in serious pain, and over the next hour his knee swelled so much he couldn't walk. His parents took him to their general physician, who then referred the boy to an orthopedic surgeon. Two weeks passed and the boy found himself in the operating room of a very humble forty-one-year-old Japanese orthopedic surgeon, Masaki Watanabe.

Dr. Watanabe had done his preoperative examination and suspected that the problem was a meniscus tear in the boy's knee. This is an extremely common problem that happens to millions of people around the world each year. Rather than doing the usual invasive surgery, which requires opening the knee and leaving a large, traumatic incision that would require days in the hospital, a cast, and months of recuperation, Dr. Watanabe did something that had never been done before. In the operating room, he made a tiny hole and passed a narrow, lighted tube with a camera attached into the knee. With this technique, which is referred to as arthroscopic surgery today, he was able to see that his diagnosis was correct. He then introduced a micro-instrument that allowed him to remove the obstructing part of the tear, hence repairing the knee. The young man was sent home the same day and was back on the basketball court in six weeks.

Again, I must reiterate that the year was 1962. To everyone in the operating room that day, not to mention the boy himself, this was simply amazing. A surgery like this had never been done before. Dr. Watanabe is widely considered the father of modern arthroscopy and by all accounts a big "C" Creative. Had he kept this surgical innovation to himself, he would have not been a big "C" Creative. What made him a big "C" Creative was that he spread the news about this minimally invasive but effective way to perform surgery, and he mentored and trained other physicians in the technique. Ultimately, he would revolutionize not only orthopedic surgery but also surgery across medical specialties, with widespread implications for surgery as we know it today.

Just two years later, in 1964, the Olympics were held in Tokyo and a thirty-two-year-old Canadian orthopedic surgeon named Robert Jackson was there as his country's team physician. Jackson had heard about this "Japanese guy named Watanabe" and he decided to look him up while he was in Tokyo and ask if he could shadow him and learn from him. In the 1960s, it was a bit revolutionary for a Western doctor to take a step like this. In fact, up until 1980, this very promising area of arthroscopy was shunned by many orthopedic surgeons in the West, who thought it was impossible to do surgery through little poke holes. (And, of course, we can't ignore the financial reasons for shunning the practice. Major surgeries and prolonged hospital stays meant a lot of money for these doctors and their hospitals.)

Watanabe graciously agreed and Jackson spent the next two weeks operating with him and watching everything the Japanese doctor was doing. Dr. Jackson then returned to the University of Toronto and began spreading the news of these arthroscopic techniques throughout North America, including the United States. Along the way, he made his way to Boston, where I, newly returned from Europe, happened to be training in orthopedics. Dr. Jackson was a friend of my mentor at the time, Dr. Robert Leach, who was the chair of the Boston University and Lahey Clinic Orthopedic Program. Dr. Leach was just as open-minded and curious as Jackson and Watanabe. He always put his patients first and was looking for new and better ways to help them; he, too, began to adopt arthroscopic techniques. And it was with Dr. Leach that I did my first arthroscopy in 1979.

Thanks to Dr. Watanabe—a big "C" Creative—who changed the entire domain of surgery by educating a field of experts, I, too, became an arthroscopic surgeon. By the time I graduated from my orthopedic residency, this type of surgery was becoming more mainstream. Eventually I would be able to apply arthroscopic surgery to shoulder injuries.

What It Means to Be a Small "c" Creative

Fast-forward to 2011, when I had been practicing as a surgeon for over thirty years. By this time, I was specializing only in arthroscopic procedures, but I had further narrowed my focus to arthroscopic shoulder surgery. One day I was in my practice and a physician's assistant said that a patient was on the phone and wished to speak to me.

I responded, "Sure, but to whom will I be speaking?"

"Mario Andretti," my PA said.

I was not surprised when I heard his name. Over the years, Mario and I had formed a close relationship. We went way back, though I had known him longer than he did me! I was a senior in college when the world-famous race car driver first won the Indianapolis 500. Here was an Italian American immigrant who had become an American idol, and I was one of his staunchest fans. I never believed our paths would cross. When I had moved to the Lehigh Valley in eastern Pennsylvania and was just opening my first regional sports medicine clinic and serving as team physician for Lehigh University athletics, Mario Andretti walked into my exam room. He had married a woman from the area and settled down here, so in a way we were "neighbors." I could not believe it. After all these years, he was standing in front of me. He was handsome, polite, and charming, but what struck me most was his humble nature. I could see why he was adored by millions around the world. We soon became friends. He attended fundraising events and parties at my home, and we touched base over the phone often. To this day we speak to each other every Christmas Eve. But he never calls me at work unless there's an issue, so when he called me that day in my office, I knew it must be serious.

By this point, he had retired from professional racing but had started something called the Mario Andretti Racing Experience, where he had cars fitted with two seats and he took passengers out on an Indy track at a very high speed.

I took the call and Mario said, "I have a problem with my shoulder. You think you can look at it, doc?" (Though I had asked him to call me Emilio from the day we met, he always insisted on calling me "doc.")

Of course I agreed to take a look. As we spoke, I immediately understood why he was likely experiencing shoulder pain. You have to have very strong arms and shoulders to hold the vibrating steering wheel of a car going at high speeds, and eventually this takes its toll on the rotator cuff, which is what had happened to him.

He went on to explain that he'd had several physicians both in Indianapolis and on the West Coast look at it. They had done an MRI and explained that it was a chronic tear of the rotator cuff and there was minimal tissue present to perform the repair. Most doctors warned he might not be able to go back to high-speed driving.

Mario came over that afternoon with his previous MRI and we did some further testing. The tear was indeed chronic and retracted—however, there appeared to be some tendon that we might be able to mobilize and stitch with some new anchor techniques.

Most doctors wouldn't touch an injury like this one, because there was so little tissue present. So we had to be creative. I worked with my team, drew up some diagrams of our approach based on many surgeries I had done in the past, ran possible scenarios, and then explained the risks and the game plan to Mario. He agreed to the surgery. We took him into the operating room and we fixed his shoulder.

Mario was absolutely delighted. Within three months, he was back in a high-speed car. To this day, he has no problems with his shoulder.

What I did for him falls under the category of small "c" creative. I wasn't trying to change the domain of orthopedic surgery; that domain had been changed in 1962 by Dr. Watanabe and those who came after him. I just used the tools within that domain at a creative level. I was also not trying to persuade a field of experts to change their minds. I was simply one expert within the domain, acting creatively.

Using Small "c" Creativity to Become Fully Human

What does creativity have to do with becoming fully human? And how does being a small "c" creative affect our humanity? Creativity is central to and required for one's humanity, but so are one's morality, intellect, spirituality, and relationships.

The Components of Being Fully Human

1. Intellect: You must be intellectually curious. You have to study and understand your area of expertise as well as areas outside your expertise. You need to work hard and gather the tools, skills, and intelligence required to perfect your techniques.
2. Relationship: Whether it's significant others, family members, friends, coworkers, customers, clients, or acquaintances—humans

are constantly engaging with each other. There is nothing we do that can escape our relationship with other human beings. Humans are also part of the creative process and benefit from creativity. Keeping humans front and center of all creativity makes us more creative, and therefore, more fully human.

3. Morality: You must have a sense of right and wrong, of working for the benefit, rather than the harm, of others.
4. Spirituality: It doesn't matter who or what you believe in, but being a creative requires that you keep something "bigger" than yourself in mind when you begin to create. Some people call this the muse; some people call this God, Jesus, Buddha, Christ, Krishna, or the Universe. No matter what you call it, creativity requires a level of surrender to ideas, thoughts, and inspiration from beyond yourself.

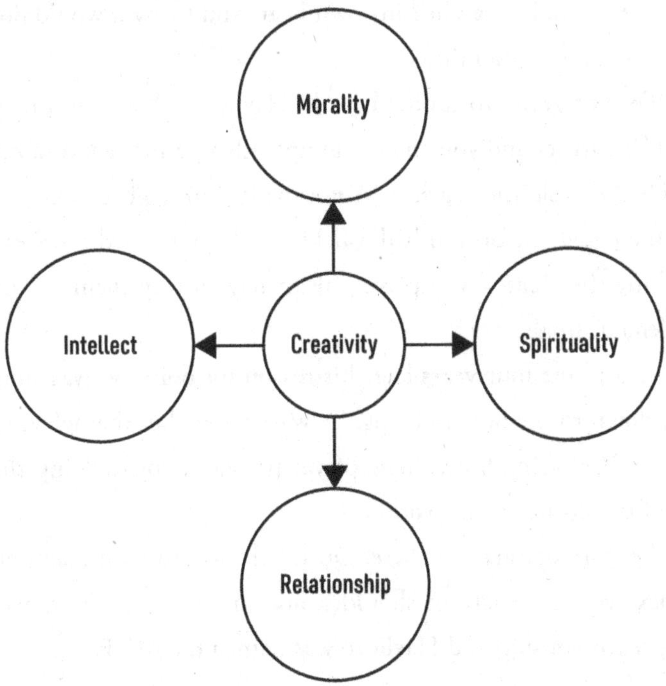

Take, for example, my mentor in orthopedics and sports medicine, Dr. Leach. He taught me a lot of things, but one of the most important things he taught me about being a creative physician was the importance of developing a relationship with my patients. Now, for context, Dr. Leach was a major pioneer in his field. Like Dr. Watanabe, Dr. Leach was a big "C" Creative. He is considered one of the fathers of what we now call sports medicine. When I was Dr. Leach's chief resident, he was the team physician for the Boston Celtics. In 1973, the Celtics were playing in the Eastern Conference NBA playoff finals, and a key player, John Havlicek, collided with another player and separated the shoulder of his dominant shooting arm. Everyone in the stands and on the bench wanted Dr. Leach to get him back on the court as soon as possible. Dr. Leach could have shot Havlicek's arm with Novocain before the next game to get him through the playoffs and guarantee a win for the Celtics. Although everyone urged Dr. Leach to do so, he searched his own heart and knew it would do more harm than good (morality).

"I'm not going to do it," he told Havlicek. "You could tear your shoulder further and you could end up with a permanent disability."

He then told the coaches, "You can't let him go back in."

The papers in Boston had a field day. Fans blamed Dr. Leach for benching the Celtics' star player, ultimately costing them the Eastern Conference finals.

He told me four years later his reason for doing so was simple. It came down to the human being. "Always remember that when you do the very best thing for a single player [patient], you're doing the best thing for your team [the world]."

The story doesn't end there. Dr. Leach worked with Havlicek over the next year to rehab his shoulder, and in 1974 the Celtics won the NBA championship and Havlicek was named the MVP.

Dr. Leach—one of the most creative physicians I ever met—taught me the importance of morality (doing no harm), intellect (thinking deeply about an issue and running through all the scenarios), and forming a deep relationship (caring deeply about the whole person). Finally, he taught me the importance of keeping spirituality (answering to a higher being) at the forefront of my mind. He was one of the first people I witnessed who had become more fully human due to the power of creativity. I was so fortunate to have been in Boston at the right time. I often say that so much of what happened in my life I owe to luck, time, and a power greater than me. Had it not been for big "C" Creatives like Watanabe, Jackson, and Leach, I would not have discovered arthroscopic surgery, let alone the creative process, which they first demonstrated for me.

Jump-Start Your Creativity

Writing prompts for your journal:

- What areas spark your curiosity? Are you interested in learning more about these areas?
- How much time do you dedicate to thinking about your relationships? How can you better serve your audience, customer, family, friends, or the world?
- How often do you consider your own morality—that is, your sense of right and wrong? How much of your creative mind do you use to solve problems for others?
- How much of a role does spirituality play in your life? Do you consider it essential to your creativity?

CHAPTER 3

The Creative Process

In the previous two chapters, I discussed how creativity affects us on a personal level. Creativity is a vehicle that allows a person to become more fully human. But there are many components to a human's personhood—a person's personality; how their early-childhood, or even in utero, experience affects and forms them; how their societal, cultural, and spiritual upbringing influences their worldview; and, of course, their intellect and natural talents and proclivities. And these can all be further affected by their access to education, healthcare, or even proper nutrition. So much affects who we are and why we are the way we are. Epigeneticists, neuroscientists, biologists, anthropologists, psychologists, philosophers, and even poets have tried to make sense of what makes us human for centuries. I will not even pretend to dive into what makes up our personalities, temperaments, or proclivities. Many experts have argued that the personality is something we are born with and will remain unchanged, while others have said that our personalities are merely constructs of our subconscious mind as a means to protect us from early traumas. These subsequently become "part of who we are" but can change with therapy and self-actualization. Since this is not a book on neuroscience or psychology but rather one that focuses on creativity, I will let the neuroscientists figure out how a person's brain works to create one's personality. My main concern is how to work with each of our unique personalities to develop as a creative person.

From Linear to Nonlinear

As mentioned in the introduction, the creative process exists in five stages, which serve as the framework for this book. In the chapters that follow, I present these five stages in a linear manner because that is how they're easiest to understand and apply. But, in reality, the creative process is anything but linear. When we are thinking creatively, there is an interplay of stages and none exist in isolation from the rest. The mechanism of creativity is a complex machine of moving parts.

When we talk about "stages" in the creative process, we really should be using the word "condition" instead of "stage," as Scott Jeffrey points out in *Creativity Revealed*: "When conditions are appropriate, manifestation (creativity) unfolds. The stages of creativity do not *cause* creativity; rather, they represent some of the conditions necessary for creativity to emerge."[1] In other words, when we are engaged in the creative process, these five conditions are functioning together in order for creativity to happen.

The goal of the creative process is not gaining expertise or proficiency in a particular area. Many of us are familiar with the 10,000-hour rule that author Malcolm Gladwell popularized in his book *Outliers*. The idea was first championed by Anders Ericsson, who

---

1. Scott Jeffrey, *Creativity Revealed: Discovering the Source of Inspiration* (Creative Crayon Publishers, 2008), 42.

argued that experts are made with time, through a linear approach of repetition and efficiency. Most miss his fundamental argument, however: that it's not the 10,000 hours alone that make someone an expert but rather the quality of the time and the incremental improvements that are made every day. For example, if you just showed up to the track every day and jogged for an hour, and you didn't change anything else about your routine, you would not become an elite runner after 10,000 hours of going around the track. Expertise at something like running can be attained only if you keep improving, add resistance, and develop certain muscles, and even then, there is no guarantee that the 10,000 hours will work. I can spend 10,000 hours playing tennis, but that won't make me Roger Federer. What makes Federer "Federer the Tennis Expert" is how he practices during this time.

Becoming an expert creative is not a linear process but rather an irregular one. In making *Guernica*, Pablo Picasso did not begin with a single sketch and then follow specific, linear steps to transfer that sketch to his giant canvas. Instead, he came to a decision regarding a figure for which he had made a sketch and then changed it. In fact, he made these changes right on the final canvas. He ended up creating heads that looked more primitive after visiting a museum and being inspired by primitive sculptures. Picasso said, "I almost never know where I'm going until I get there." It is common to hear creative people say, "I could not have planned that in advance."

The Five Stages of the Creative Process

As mentioned, variations of the creative process have been developed by notable academics such as Mihaly Csikszentmihalyi, Keith Sawyer, and many others. Graham Wallas's four-stage framework remains the foundation, and I have used this framework as the basis for my discussion of the creative process in this book. I have also added a fifth stage, implementation, because to "make" a finished product requires creativity as well and is sometimes the most challenging stage of the process.

Each stage includes a set of functions, or what I call Jobs to Be Done (JTBD), which need to be carried out in order for the process to work. The number of JTBD varies by stage.

Jobs to Be Done (JTBD) by Stage

For each stage of the creative process, there are certain Jobs to Be Done in order to move forward on the path. Some of these jobs are functional. For example, in preparation, some Jobs to Be Done are researching, such as reading up on your topic, visiting areas related to your topic, and talking to and interviewing others to gain further knowledge. Some of these jobs are emotional. For example, in the incubation stage, you will need to "let go" and "trust the process."

The Jobs to Be Done (JTBD) are broken down into both the functional JTBD and the mental JTBD. The functional jobs are equivalent to a set of instructions, a road map of sorts that you will need to follow in order to execute each stage. The mental JTBD are the mindsets, or mental hats, to be worn during each stage. These mental hats can be thought of as set patterns of behavior for that particular process stage. These patterns of behavior can be thought of as archetypes or universal mental mindsets.

For example, part of my becoming a surgeon required the "job" of studying and knowing anatomy. Then it required that I learn how to operate. To become a sculptor, I had various jobs to do as well—I had to study anatomy, learn how to draw and sculpt, and learn about what tools and methods and techniques to use. For each JTBD there is a road map. This set of instructions provides a road map (not a destination) for you while you are in search of a creative product.

The stages and the corresponding JTBD needed for each stage can be summarized in a linear fashion as follows:

Stage	Jobs to Be Done (JTBD)		
Stage 1 Preparation	**Job 1** • Spot the need or opportunity • Identify the problem • Develop a strategy for a solution to the problem	**Job 2** • Gather information and materials directly related to the problem • Acquire knowledge directly related to the problem	**Job 3** • Gather information potentially related to the problem
Stage 2 Incubation	**Job 1** • Higher (sub) consciousness working on problem resolution • Ideas and their connections have to permeate • Cannot be forced/happens on its own		
Stage 3 Insight	**Job 1** • Producing ideas • Subconscious → conscious	**Job 2** • Integrating ideas • "Connecting the dots"	
Stage 4 Evaluation	**Job 1** • Choosing best ideas	**Job 2** • Integrating best ideas	
Stage 5 Implementation	**Job 1** • Externalize best integrated ideas—"make"	**Job 2** • Release to the world	

Stages and Mindsets

Each of the five stages of the creative process also calls for cultivation of a particular mindset, which is needed to progress through that stage. Throughout the book, I will refer to these mindsets as "archetypes," each corresponding to a particular stage of the creative process, based on the personal qualities and behaviors needed to perform the JTBD of that stage.

The stages with their corresponding mindsets are as follows (I will go into depth on each archetype throughout the book):

Stage	Mindset
Preparation	The Learner
Incubation	The Voyager
Insight	The Thinker
Evaluation	The Analyst
Implementation	The Builder

In order to be a creative—whether with a big "C" or small "c"—one must become emotionally ready and adopt a particular set of behaviors to produce the optimal conditions to execute the creative process.

The stages and the corresponding archetypes needed for each stage can be summarized as follows:

The Creative Process: Archetypes for Each Stage

Stage	Archetype	Purpose	Behavioral qualities
Stage 1: Preparation	The Learner	Learn	• Humility • Commitment • Looking for truth • Focus • Enthusiasm • Allowing • Adaptive • Openness • Patience • Gratitude
↓ **Stage 2: Incubation**	The Voyager	Think about nothing	• Allowing • Adaptive • Openness • Patience • Gratitude
↓ **Stage 3: Insight**	The Thinker	Allow creative ideas to move into conscious mind	• Faith in higher power • Knowing of something greater than oneself
↓ **Stage 4: Evaluation**	The Analyst	Validate creative ideas	• Dedication • Skills and knowledge
↓ **Stage 5: Implementation**	The Builder	Develop innovation from creative ideas	• Detail orientation

Behaviors Are the Greatest Determinant of Creativity

When creativity is present, the five stages (conditions)—preparation, incubation, insight, evaluation, and implementation—are functioning to set the stage for creativity to take place. And at the foundation of each stage (condition) is a set of behaviors—which are distinct from personality. Again, as I said in the introduction, creativity is not a trait, personality type, or "gift" or "talent." Creativity is dependent on a set of behaviors that can be learned. Creativity isn't some elusive innate gift that some are "lucky" to have while others don't. It is literally a mindset that with lifelong practice can be developed. In each chapter, we will explore in depth the set of behaviors that is required for each stage.

Jump-Start Your Creativity

Writing prompts for your journal:

- How has this chapter's discussion of the creative process changed the way you think of creativity?
- What are some personality traits you possess? If you were to describe yourself to someone (or they were to describe you), how might they describe you?
- What creative behaviors do you already practice, even if you would not have identified as a "creative type" before?

PART 2

The Creative Process at Work

CHAPTER 4

Stage 1: Preparation

Creativity requires developing a new idea or a new way of looking at something. It also requires that we find ways to develop, understand, and communicate these new ideas. But before we can produce these new ideas or generate some "product," whether it's a piece of art, an innovation, or a business, we need to prepare.

JTBD 1: Find and Solve a Challenging Problem

All around us people are looking for creative solutions to present-day problems. The answers we are looking for are rarely easy—or if they're easy, they're difficult to agree upon. Ask five different people how to solve climate change, and you will get five different answers. Ask five different people how to end racism, and you'll no doubt have at least one person who doesn't even think it's a problem. What may seem simple at the outset can become more complex the further you dive into the subject matter. As a surgeon, I can attest to the fact that seemingly simple routine surgeries can turn complicated quickly. Over the years, I had to think creatively on the spot—running through various scenarios and searching for the right solution in the moment in order to save a life. Sometimes challenges that require creative solutions present themselves quite obviously. Other times, we have to struggle a bit to discover what the real challenge is. We ask ourselves, *Am I trying to solve a problem to address the current situation? Or am I trying to find the cause of the problem?*

Often there appear to be multiple solutions. You can apply your past experience to generate a solution. More times than not, I had seen similar situations before in the OR, and therefore I could predict what I should do next while operating on a patient based on my past experiences. But there were times I had to act in the moment, discovering new creative solutions in real time. When you're looking for questions and answers to challenging problems, it's not like taking the SAT or MCAT. Rarely is life a multiple-choice test. When it comes to creativity, the questions are limitless, and the possible list of solutions is just as long. It's like driving through a new city with Waze turned on. As you come to roadblocks and traffic jams, you need to reroute for the most efficient route to your destination—only to find out later that while the route was neither fast nor efficient, it was exactly what you needed at the time to get through a tough spot. And once you get to your destination, you find out there were many other roads you could have taken.

Another way of saying this is: creativity requires divergent thinking.

Strategies for Finding the Solution to the Problem

Strategy is fundamental to the entire creative process. It is the organizing approach around which you undertake creative idea production and problem-solving.

Strategy is foundational to your work. There are two strategies used for creative problem-solving. I was trained in systems thinking as a systems engineer in college. Later I discovered design thinking, though it was being talked about at MIT and Stanford in the 1950s by John E. Arnold, whom some credit as being one of the first to write about what we now refer to as the science of creativity and innovation. But it really became popular in the 1990s when Tim Brown and David Kelley, the founders of IDEO, a design firm, organized their systematic approach to design using a human-centered (user-friendly) approach. They then called their methodology "design thinking" and now offer classes and certifications in the method.

Systems thinking requires you to ask the question, What problem does my idea solve? Design thinking requires you to ask, Will my user or customer like and use my idea? The strategy of systems thinking involves looking first at the whole, then at the parts that make up the whole, and finally at how the parts interact and connect. It uses analysis and synthesis. Design thinking's strategy involves a focus on the user in a solutions-based approach. This strategy allows for "testing and tweaking" of an idea or solution.

For example, when I set out to write this book, I sat down and had a strategy session with my editors. Using both approaches, we defined the problem: How do we write a book on creativity? There were innumerable books already written on the topic and even more ways to explore writing a new one. I narrowed the focus to a defined set and combination of topics based on my experiences—the chapters you see now in the table of contents. Then I set about researching and writing each chapter. Using the systems and design thinking strategies enabled me to identify the approach I would take in researching and developing the content of this book and clearly presenting the creative process to you, the reader.

Design thinking solves problems by being human-centric and relies on prototyping/testing. Systems thinking solves problems by seeing the bigger, more complex environment and how everything is connected. These two schools of thought differ in their approach and focus, and each has its own pros and cons. When we combine the two, however, we can produce more creative solutions throughout every stage of the creative process.

Systems Thinking for Creative Problem-Solving

MIT professor Jay Forrester introduced systems thinking in 1956. Systems thinking is expressed through big-picture and detailed visualization; it helps break down a big problem into its component parts and then figures out how each part affects the whole.

Systems problem-solving considers all factors involved. It can help an organization find the root cause of a problem and find a solution that addresses all the symptoms. One of the most important components of systems thinking is attention to feedback. In a business, it involves considering both management and customer feedback. This attention to cause and effect can help build better connections and relationships. It also helps make sure you don't take actions that have been counterproductive in the past. Systems thinking studies the problem extensively before arriving at a solution. It allows us to study how the different parts within the systems relate to each other. This, in turn, allows us to spot recurring patterns. Because systems thinking spends a lot of time examining the system, it can take a lot of time and create a ton of data to analyze. It's important to stay focused on the data that is applicable to the solution that is needed.

The strategy behind systems thinking involves two complementary abilities: analysis and synthesis. Analysis breaks down a system's components and functions. Synthesis creates a whole from the parts. It might examine:

- How pieces of a business are connected
- How colors in a painting are connected
- How a production line functions
- How flights at a busy airport leave on time

The basic principles of systems thinking state:

- A whole is made up of parts.
- The parts are interdependent.
- The properties of the parts are detected only when looking first at the whole.
- The whole can sometimes be greater than the parts (1 + 1 = 3).
- It is a nonlinear type of thinking that allows for other perspectives.

Another way of defining systems thinking is that it is a holistic approach—that is, it considers the whole. When one is treating the body, it's important to think of the whole body. One can't simply study a single aspect of the body and not consider its impact on the whole. Nevertheless, one needs to both understand the whole and specialize—remaining too general can mean one lacks specific knowledge of a certain area. For example, I wouldn't want a heart surgeon operating on my knee. And I wouldn't assign an orthopedic surgeon to a complex heart surgery. But I would expect both surgeons to have an understanding of the whole body.

An iceberg is often the best metaphor or visual tool to illustrate systems thinking:

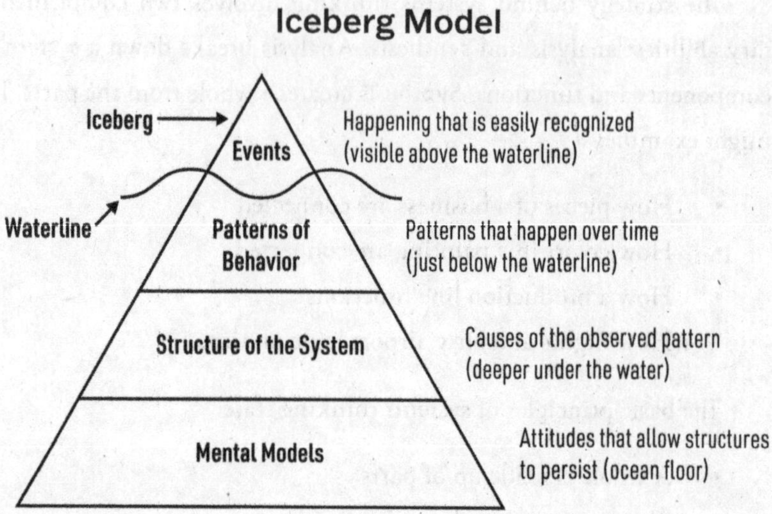

A complex world often requires our problem-solving strategies to be complex. If the problem is complex, our approach needs to consider that complexity. If you try to fix a problem by focusing only on the part that needs fixing without considering how the fix affects other systems, you may end up with new problems. Systems thinking helps us produce creative ideas by always looking at the big picture first and then working to understand how the other systems might be affected.

Let's look at the example of a seventy-year-old male being evaluated for knee replacement surgery:

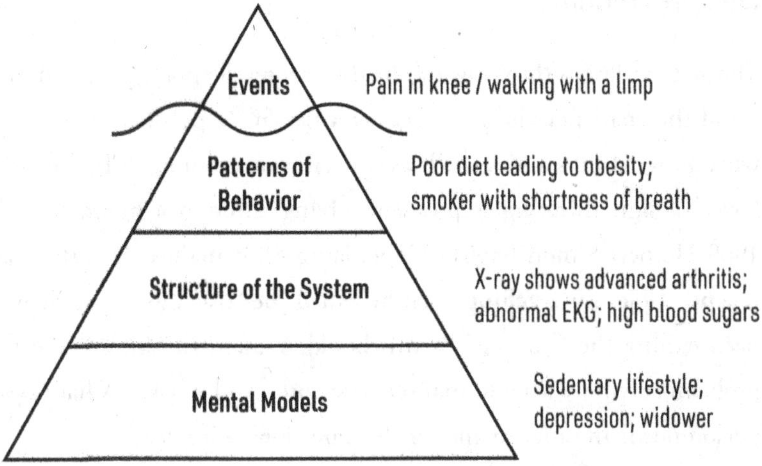

Before operating on this patient to replace his arthritic knee, the surgeon has to evaluate other systems—for example, the heart, lungs, and blood. Applying a systems thinking mindset allows the surgeon to identify potential secondary problem areas that may result from major knee surgery.

How to Apply Systems Thinking in Practice

You should observe the system and learn from it first instead of immediately imposing your own ideas or solutions. Remember that teams and teamwork are as much a part of the system as anything else, so involve others in the system. Avoid working in an isolated or competitive environment. Communicate and learn from others. Share your experiences. Listen to feedback and suggestions. Try to have individuals on your team who possess different skills and complementary knowledge. Systems thinking also allows an individual to better understand their role within a team and to understand how team members are working with each other.

Design Thinking

The goal of design thinking and its user-centered approach is to understand the challenges human users of a system or product face. It asks what a user thinks and feels. It asks what motivations and beliefs users have. Design thinking is problem-solving through a micro lens. In 1969 Herbert Simon (later a Nobel laureate) explained that there are five principles for reaching what he called the "user" (or what we have been calling the "human" in this book). Design thinking is creative problem-solving with a human-centric core. And it asks, What does a person need? In order to answer this question, you must:

- Empathize: care about your user
- Define: understand your user's needs
- Ideate: generate ideas for solutions a user would actually use
- Prototype: create a solution
- Test or assess a prototype

While design thinking focuses on the needs of the end user in order to find solutions to problems that work for them, it also allows us to continue to "test and tweak" the solution until it serves the user best.

In focusing on a specific user's point of view, however, an organization's goal may be overlooked and the larger purpose forgotten. Design thinking narrows its focus to the experience of the end user, and as a result, sometimes a gap occurs between ideas and execution. For example, if Apple had focused only on the end user—if it had provided an elegant touch screen experience with a seamless interface while ignoring costs, materials, how apps work, and software creation—we would not have an iPhone. Design thinking helps you imagine how a user will interact with a product; systems thinking gives the designers and engineers a framework and workflow so that the ideas are executed and deployed in the right part of the system—that is, the part that will allow it to thrive. If you lack continuity and interpretation, your solution will not be placed within the right part of the organization's system. This is why you need to also use the wider focus of systems thinking, which considers the entire organization, not just the user.

JTBD 2: Acquire Knowledge Directly Related to the Problem

When I set about writing a book on creativity, one of the first things I did was research and read everything I could that had already been written about the topic. Likewise, as a young surgeon, I studied medicine. Today, as a sculptor and an artist, before I begin any piece, I dive into the subject matter and learn as much as I can. Whenever we set out on a creative problem-solving pursuit, it's imperative that we take the time to do our "homework." Has this been done before? The only way to find this out is to study the past. The old saying "There is nothing new under the sun" is true. There is a funny reel on the internet of a teenager sitting in her car and wondering, "Why don't they come up with one phone just to keep at the house—and whoever is home answers it?" If you're older than twenty, you might be thinking, *Is she for real? Is this a joke?* She thinks she's discovered the idea for a landline, which almost every house in the United States had until mobile phones took over. But, as a young person, she had no idea, no concept that these dinosaur phones once existed. So many people think they have discovered something novel, only to find out that it's already been done (again and again and again). But that's not always a bad thing. Knowing what's been done allows us to expand and explore even more.

As a visual artist, I've spent many hours reading and studying European sculpture and painting, beginning with the cave drawings in France and continuing through the Italian Renaissance and Paris at the start of the last century. My experience in management science was preceded by my study of Peter Drucker, Michael Porter, and Clay Christensen. My creativity as an orthopedic surgeon rests on the shoulders of Sir John Charnley, Anthony DePalma, and Robert Leach. And you may think that there is some mythical genius "artist" who doesn't have to study others and who can simply go off and create without learning about what's gone before them, but I assure you that even Mozart dedicated time each day to studying the work of others. In one of his published letters to a friend he wrote, "People err who think my art comes easily to me. I assure you dear friend, nobody has devoted so much time and thought to composition as I. There is not a famous master whose music I have not industriously studied through many times."

If you find that something has already been done, don't just throw up your hands. Research carefully what has been said and done by others, because that is how you can determine what areas haven't been explored yet. Ask yourself: *Are there new ways of looking at this issue? Are there more nuanced approaches to the work? What are the latest discoveries?* The only way to find this out is to spend some time studying the subject.

Focused Study on the Subject

No matter what I am creating, I try to learn everything relevant to the problem (project, process). This requires much thinking and study on the particular subject, be it a new business model, surgical procedure, sculpture, or something else. No matter what you're doing, research is imperative. Becoming familiar with your subject matter helps in untold ways. For example, there is a story I love about Leonardo da Vinci that I came across in Twyla Tharp's book *The Creative Habit*. Apparently, Pope Leo X felt that Leonardo was wasting time working on formulas for varnishes, thinking that Leonardo would make better use of his time by actually painting. But Leonardo understood what the pope did not. As Tharp put it, "The better you know the nuts and bolts of your craft, the more fully you can express your talents. The great painters are incomparable draftsmen. They also know how to mix their own paint, grind it, put in the fixative; no task is too small to be worthy of their attention."

I agree with Tharp that, as she says, "What all these (creative) people have in common is that they have mastered the underlying skills of their creative domain, and built their creativity on the solid foundation of those skills."[1]

It is important to learn what has already been done. Even Homer couldn't have written his *Iliad* and *Odyssey* without fully becoming a student of the oral tradition and folklore of his people. All the great writers set about studying their subject matter. Hemingway sat in the bullfighting arena. Steinbeck couldn't have written *The Grapes of Wrath* without researching and living among the people he was writing about—migrant workers. When he was asked to write about what was going on during World War II, he worked as a war correspondent and studied the neglected parts of the war by immersing himself among the different people affected. He wrote with such clarity and precision because he was on the ground with the people whose stories he was telling. He once said, "Three hours of writing require twenty hours of preparation."[2] (I am finding as I write this book that he is not far off. It takes hours of research and careful note-taking, drawing, and planning before I even sit down to write.) Georgia O'Keeffe studied the place she lived. Every day she painted the area around her home in New Mexico. Over and over she would paint the ladder leaning against her home, paying attention to the shadow it cast at different times of day.

---

1. Twyla Tharp, *The Creative Habit: Learn It and Use It for Life* (Simon & Schuster, 2003), 7.

2. John Steinbeck, *Steinbeck: A Life in Letters*, ed. Elaine Steinbeck and Robert Wallsten (Penguin, 1989), 67.

No matter what you're trying to achieve, you need to become familiar with your subject and stay up-to-date in your field of study. Warren Buffett, one of the world's richest men and most successful investors, reads six newspapers a day. He reads the full financial reports of the companies he invests in. He is constantly learning and adapting his strategies based on the new information he discovers each and every day. A creative person must never be complacent or think that they have it all figured out.

Focus on Skills to Achieve the Task at Hand

And while having all this information is great, it's useless if you don't do anything with it. At some point, a researcher has to stop living among their subjects and researching their theories. Eventually they have to sit at their desk and begin to write. The marketer has to open up Instagram and sift through photos and videos to write the social media post. The investor has to buy or sell their stocks. The accountant has to open Excel. The gardener has to start digging and planting. This is where skills and practice come in.

Building creativity on a solid foundation of skill gives us the wherewithal to execute a creative idea. The great composers are usually dazzling musicians. The great sculptors are often superb draftsmen. The great architects are both excellent drafters and businesspeople. The great surgeons are in love with anatomy. The great leaders are marvelous storytellers. The great chefs have better knife skills than anyone else. Steven Pressfield, in in his seminal book *The War of Art*, puts it this way: "The professional respects his craft. He does not consider himself superior to it. He recognizes the contributions of those who have gone before him. He apprentices himself to them . . . He knows that by toiling beside the front door of technique, he leaves room for genius to enter by the back."[3]

---

3. Steven Pressfield, *The War of Art* (Rugged Land, 2002), 79–80.

Deliberate Practice

You can't become the fastest person in the world by going out and running around your block every day until you reach 10,000 hours. You can't become the world's best investor just by getting up and trading stocks every day. You can't have a spectacular garden simply by watering it over and over for 10,000 hours. The time you spend is only part of the equation. You must practice, challenge yourself, and seek to improve every day. Great musicians don't just practice the same song over and over. They tackle more difficult chord progressions, and they seek out partners and coaches to help them through complicated processes. Deliberate practice for a surgeon is not doing the same shoulder operation the same way over and over again. It means taking on shoulder conditions a bit beyond the norm, but ones you can still master with planning, concentration, and feedback from your peers. It means never being comfortable. It means always working to get better.

The crucial aspect of Anders Ericsson's research on excellence is not that experts log more hours of practice; rather, *it's that experts practice differently*. For their 1993 paper for the *Psychological Review*, "The Role of Deliberate Practice in the Acquisition of Expert Performance," Ericsson and his colleagues Ralf Krampe and Clemens Tesch-Romer extensively studied experts in their respective realms and created a theoretical framework for what truly results in improved performances.

Their article argues that those who engage in deliberate practice constantly stretch themselves, focusing on one area of performance—particularly an area in which they don't already excel. That is, they identify their own weaknesses or areas of opportunity for growth. A runner with strong legs, for example, may focus on their core and breathwork. Another form of deliberate practice is one's motivation or desire to persist in the face of challenges. It's like the old story of Larry Bird getting up and dribbling a basketball down the street and putting in extra hours on the court. He was practicing even when his coaches weren't looking. Bird became well known for his ball-handling skills and had what he called the "someone else is dribbling" mentality that his high school coach, Jim Jones, had taught him. He used to tell Bird that there was someone else out there practicing, which inspired Bird to keep going even when he wanted to stop. Those who engage in deliberate practice also need and look for feedback. They don't see it as criticism—they see it as a means of getting better. They also don't shrink, get defensive, or give up when they are told they need to improve. Criticism motivates them to dig even deeper.

Eventually, you, too, after years and years of practicing, tweaking, and improving, will become a specialist. Which can be a great thing, until it's not . . .

Generalist Versus Specialist

After ten years of study, you may become a specialist, but your focus might have become so narrow that you miss the big picture. To maximize your creativity, it's ideal to learn as much as you can in a given field while cultivating a knowledge of other fields. While being an expert or a specialist is helpful, being a generalist in other fields will give you untold advantages as well.

As your knowledge gets deeper, it also has to get broader. Just as you needed focused study when you set out on your pursuit, at some point you will also need to study topics that are adjacent to your problem. It's there that you might find some new solutions. When I worked with new orthopedic surgical implants, my knowledge in material science, which I had acquired in engineering school many years prior, allowed me to converse and be creative with the design engineers.

Creative ideas that go on to become innovations usually result from a combination of ideas developed by a combination of people with a combination of skill sets. Sometimes, as we work to increase and improve our skills in our field, we are led into different areas and new horizons.

In Steve Jobs's 2005 commencement address at Stanford University, he explained that as a nineteen-year-old, he had dropped out of Reed College but decided to take a class in typography, a skill that would seem to have no practical value at the time. When Jobs connected the dots years later, he realized that this class was responsible for the world-class typography in the Macintosh computer.

That is the beauty of this stage of preparation—you really have no idea how all your knowledge and skills will coalesce and come in handy in the future. When I was acquiring skills in systems engineering, I had no idea how they would affect me in orthopedic surgery, how both these focused areas of study would lead to the development of a healthcare management company, or how all my studies and work over my lifetime would result in my experience as a sculptor and painter today.

JTBD 3: Seek and Gather Information Seemingly Unrelated to the Problem

While you're focusing on your subject matter, honing your skills, and understanding other areas related to the subject matter, you also need to be aware of all the apparently unrelated information in the environment, which can provide potential solutions for your creative problems.

In 1941, George de Mestral, an engineer and inventor, went on a walk with his dog in the Swiss Alps. Burs were stuck all over de Mestral's dog and also on his pants. Dog owners never notice how cleverly burs are designed; they just get annoyed. De Mestral was annoyed but also intrigued. He saved one of the burs and looked at it closely under a microscope. At the end of each sharp spine, he noticed a tiny hook. These hooks snagged on fur and clothing. Looking at them closely gave de Mestral the idea of putting spines with hooks on one side of fabric and tiny loops on the other piece, creating Velcro.[4]

If we are going to be more creative, we have to act on unexpected opportunities. In order to produce creative solutions, we have to be open to accidents, mistakes, and the unexpected.

The Preparation Archetype: The Learner

As I mentioned earlier, every stage in the creative process requires us to embody a different archetype. Wearing this particular hat entails adopting certain patterns of behavior for that particular process stage. The archetype for the preparation stage is the Learner. The Learner is just what the name implies—a professional student with a beginner's mindset who is on a mission to gather as much information as possible from themselves and the world around them, as well as acquire new skills along the way. The behaviors a Learner exhibits are described below.

Humility and Openness

The Learner loves knowledge for knowledge's sake. They are open to all kinds of information and feedback. The Learner is humble and seeks counsel, direction, and information from others around them. They don't think they know it all. To this end, the Learner works hard to connect with others who may help them answer some of their questions. In doing so, they show an openness of mind. They're not arrogant with the "I know." They don't let ego get in the way. The Learner is brave enough to go against the existing field of experts when they are searching for the truth. The truth, as we'll see later, is more important than the validation of experts. This requires curiosity—or what Zen Buddhism calls a "beginner's mind."

---

4. "Our Story," accessed December 7, 2025, Velcro.com.

Commitment and Devotion

The Learner knows that creative work takes a long time, in some cases years. The more prepared we are, the deeper we can dive into our field and the better our chances are of being creative. Einstein's theory of relativity came about only after a deep study of physics for decades. Some say it took him ten years from the outset of his first question to publish his theory of relativity, but in reality it took years of study before that as well. Tolstoy took ten years to write *War and Peace.* It took Marcel Proust thirteen years to write *In Search of Lost Time.* Sometimes creating something takes time. If we know this and we can commit to spend the time it takes, we can muster our devotion during the days we don't feel as motivated to continue.

Inner Alignment with Something Greater—Searching for Truth

A Learner knows they aren't the smartest person in the room. In fact, they know they are not the most important one either. Rather, they understand they are just part of something bigger, which is working through them on their quest for truth. Even Albert Einstein believed in something more powerful than himself when he said, "The most beautiful and profound emotion we can experience is the sensation of the mystical. It is the source of all true science."

Patience and Grit

A Learner has to be patient, with themselves, the material, and others. Sometimes the truth emerges after an experience that is utterly frustrating. It requires both patience and grit to see through these dark times. Often, it's only after the Learner has pushed their mind to the limit and exhausted all possible answers to the question that the answer suddenly emerges. Grit helps those who possess or cultivate it reach great heights, in all manner of disciplines.

I'd posit that the principle that grit is a virtue is part of the very fabric of American society. Indeed, this country was founded on the notion that you can achieve anything with enough hard work and tenacity. This is what I call old-school grit. It's defined by a firmness of character and the ability to withstand hardships.

Over the last few years, new thinking about grit has emerged and made its way into creative circles. Angela Duckworth's 2016 book *Grit* defined the quality as "perseverance and passion for long-term goals."[5] This type of grit requires both the will to keep going when the going gets tough and a devotion to striving for a desired result. The secret to achievement, she argues, is not talent. Talent in part determines how fast we improve at a skill, but grit, a special blend of passion and persistence, is what truly drives us toward mastery. This passion and perseverance are oriented toward long-term goals: things that cannot be learned or achieved overnight. People who have grit are able to maintain their determination and motivation over long periods of time despite experiencing failure and adversity. In her years of research, Duckworth found that it wasn't always the highly gifted people who most often found long-term success. It was actually the people who showed traits of being both passionate about pursuing success and perseverant in making it happen. In other words, she showed that superior intelligence isn't always the key to success. Passion and tenacity can win over natural intellect.

So it's not falling in love but staying in love that allows the real magic to happen. For people who are creative, maintaining equal parts passion and perseverance is vital. The creative process can be very

---

5. Angela Duckworth, *Grit: The Power of Passion and Perseverance* (Scribner, 2016), 8.

difficult and frustrating, and setbacks are to be expected. Patience and grit allow us to endure. And in the process, these two qualities build our character and make us better human beings in all aspects of our lives.

Accessing the Flow State

Scholars get into flow. Mihaly Csikszentmihalyi, father of the concept, said, "Flow is being completely involved in an activity for its own sake. The ego falls away. Time flies."[6] Angela Duckworth further argues that, for most experts, deliberate practice and flow go hand in hand, though not necessarily at the same time. A common mantra used by those who coach high-caliber clients or athletes is "Deliberate practice is for preparation. Flow is for performance."

So how does flow relate to creativity? I'd say that flow is the mental state of being completely present and fully immersed in a task; it is a strong contributor to creativity and sets the Learner up for the entire creative process. At any point in time, the creative person will experience the state of flow in every stage as they begin to dive deeper into the work. Many people describe the flow state as being "fully alive" or as feeling like time doesn't exist. In other words, they feel more fully human, unbound and untethered by the constraints of the world. Another way of viewing flow is as surrendering. After a number of years, whether I was in an art studio, a planning meeting, or an operating room, I would at times achieve a calm state driven by intuition rather than conscious effort. This was often the case in the operating room. For example, after years of having done knee surgery, I would enter the operating room with a degree of self-control and insight that is hard for me to explain and was certainly not present in my training or early years of practice.

---

6. Mihaly Csikszentmihalyi, *Flow: The Psychology of Optimal Experience* (Harper & Row, 1990), 71.

Creative Actions and Behaviors Key to Preparation

Once you've put on the Learner hat and adopted the traits and behaviors of a scholar, you're going to have to rely on certain techniques and practices—tools of the preparation trade, if you will—that will serve you in this stage.

The Power of Visualization

Whether you are trying something new for the very first time or heading out for your ten thousandth time around the track, one way to increase your confidence is through visualization. Visualization has always fed my imagination. The night before I was scheduled to perform a knee operation, I would visualize a successful replacement of the knee. I pictured the scene as if I were there—I could see in my mind's eye the layout and equipment in the room. I familiarized myself with the location of all the nurses and physician's assistants in the room as well as the patient on the operating room table, with the anesthesiologist near the patient's head. I pictured taking the knife in my hand and making the initial incision. I then saw myself making the successive bone cuts and implanting the prosthesis. Finally, I visualized the wound closure and dressing application. My focus during this visualization exercise was always on a successful operation, never on one in which complications could occur.

This process is very similar to what a quarterback does. Prior to stepping out on the field, he envisions throwing his first pass and connecting with his receivers. Gymnasts and dancers close their eyes and rehearse their entire routine without moving a muscle. A writer can sit and stare out a window and imagine how an entire chapter will play out before putting their pen to paper.

In 1967, alpine skier Jean-Claude Killy of France needed a ligament reconstruction. Back then, it took nine to ten months to recover from such an operation. But Killy didn't have that much time; he was supposed to compete in the Olympics in less than a year. During that time, he could do rehab, but he wasn't permitted to put on skis because he would most likely blow his knee out again if he did so before he was fully rehabilitated. Killy obeyed the doctor's orders. While he couldn't physically practice, he knew he could still visualize skiing the courses. So he envisioned his races over and over. In his mind's eye, he traveled the courses, gate by gate, turn by turn, noting every twist, pole placement, and body posture. He went on to win triple gold in the alpine events (downhill, slalom, and giant slalom) in the 1968 Grenoble Olympics and is now considered one of the greatest alpine skiers in history.

Visualizing outcomes can increase your competence. Seeing yourself succeed helps you believe that it can and will happen. Visualization helps you practice success. When you imagine every step in an event or activity going well, you get your mind and body ready to take those steps in real life.

Remember to focus on what you want to happen—not on what you don't want to happen.

Drawing, Photography, Flowcharts, and Note-Taking

I have found over the years that people can become more creative through drawing—even those who would never think of themselves as artists. It's a human instinct to pick up a pencil or a pen to draw. Even the earliest humans expressed themselves through drawing on cave walls. I have found it improves my efficiency and efficacy during the creative process. I think of it as active thinking. Drawing, especially in the first three stages of the creative process, helps us visualize and explore the problem we're trying to solve. Whenever I am trying to explain something to someone, I pull out a pen and a piece of paper and draw. I had a colleague who was a systems engineer who drew with stick figures, but she was effective in demonstrating what she was trying to convey with even the most rudimentary of drawings. They don't have to be elaborate. It's simply a vehicle for both expressing and recording ideas.

Many people carry small journals with them and jot down ideas everywhere they go. I have a little book where I, too, jot down ideas and play with them through drawings. If drawing isn't your thing, there is always photography. Most of us have phones that now serve as an extra appendage to our bodies. We're never too far from them and we can quickly take a picture of something that inspires us or that will serve our project, and we can create a file to store all the photos in one space.

When I was a systems engineer, we lived and died by flowcharts. Anyone can tell a story through a flowchart. I had big whiteboards in my office where several flowcharts were drawn, which expressed a process I was trying to work out with my colleagues. Even now, as I am writing this book, I am relying on flowcharts to move from one idea to the next. I often write my ideas on Post-its, so I can move them around as needed.

All of these ideas can be used as tools for brainstorming. Get a bunch of people in a room and crank out as many ideas on the subject as you can and throw them up on the whiteboards. Get all your ideas out as fast as you can. Then eliminate the bad ones. You can have a thousand ideas, but maybe only one or two could actually work. Maybe it takes combining ideas for one to work. The key is to get the ideas out of your head and on some form of paper. You've often heard of famous people who say they discovered an idea at a restaurant or bar, and what did they do? They wrote it on a napkin. Paul Newman jotted down his now-famous vinaigrette salad dressing recipe for a friend one night over dinner. The friend framed it—having a hunch that it was something special they never wanted to part with and never knowing that the recipe would one day turn into a bottle that has made over $500 million for charity. You never know, you might make a small idea take off by simply writing it down, drawing it out, or elaborating on it with flowcharts.

Team-Building, Borrowing, Stealing, and Interacting with Others

We're all familiar with the romanticized ideal of the solo artist, ruminating in their studio, who creates masterpieces in isolation. Or the writer who holes themselves up in a room for a year and emerges with a beautiful novel. We love this idea of one person against the world: the starving poet, the mad scientist, the solo painter, the heroic inventor who works with nothing but their intelligence and then creates these incredible breakthroughs. You'll find lots of lore and legends about these lone creative geniuses. But the fact of the matter is that very few of those people exist. Even take an extreme example like poet Emily Dickinson or novelist Marcel Proust, both of whom were famously reclusive. Dickinson most likely suffered from social anxiety, and, yes, she spent the last twenty years of her life never leaving her family's property. But we also now know that she exchanged a massive volume of letters with relatives and friends, showing a true interest in their lives and maintaining a lively connection with them. Not necessarily what you'd expect of a recluse. On the other hand, there was Marcel Proust, the French novelist who wrote *In Search of Lost Time* and is considered to be one of the most influential authors of the twentieth century. He spent the last seventeen years of his life as a virtual recluse. He rarely left the soundproof walls of his Paris apartment or his sunless writing studio where he kept the windows shut. But even he, in an earlier life, was a social climber.

In reality, creativity is a team sport. Whether it's taking inspiration from a friend's letter when penning a poem or actually engaging in a group effort with others to achieve a goal, no one truly creates alone. In business, a team with diverse experiences that is also efficient in sharing their knowledge is a winning recipe for the discovery of groundbreaking innovations. Even so-called genius inventors all had incredible support teams around them, and the success they achieved is attributable more to the strength of the group than to the genius of one individual.

There's one story about a solitary creative genius that a lot of people have heard and return to repeatedly: that of Thomas Edison. He was the man behind some of the major inventions of the nineteenth century, like the phonograph, the alkaline battery, and the first video camera. He's also credited with creating the light bulb, but in reality he perfected and refined the idea, vastly improving its longevity. Edison certainly didn't sit alone in his shop for 10,000 hours trying this filament and that one and eventually landing on the idea of his light bulb. In fact, twenty-two people invented incandescent lamps before Edison even filed for his first patent for that particular technology.

Edison was a brilliant scientist; there's no question about that. He was also a very hardworking man and was devoted to his craft. Though we know him for the products he created and his role in ushering in the age of electricity, perhaps his most important achievement was the creation of a special place midway between Philadelphia and New York, in Menlo Park.

At his Menlo research park, Edison hired individuals with varying skill sets. Some of them were machinists. Some of them were physicists. Some of them were engineers. This team called themselves the Muckers, a slang term that soldiers used for their comrades who worked, lived, fought, and died alongside each other. Edison's Muckers were responsible for a lot of the breakthroughs and improvements that you hear credited to Edison all the time. As his career progressed, Edison himself spent a lot of time dealing with clients, speaking to the press, and entertaining potential investors. The Muckers were the ones tinkering, discovering, and perfecting. They worked on separate projects in the same room. They ate lunch together. They spent time together. They shared jokes and ideas. Their insights cross-pollinated and led to true innovations. They also had no problem "stealing" ideas from other industries far beyond their walls and incorporating them into products they were developing. The Muckers were the electricity providing the power to Edison's light bulb, so to speak, but the public mostly heard about a single individual, Edison, thereby supporting the romantic, mythological notion of the lone genius. In fact, when people spoke of Edison, they were really referring to a collective noun.

We see very similar situations in the world of art. Michelangelo did not paint the Sistine Chapel by himself. Thinking in practical terms, consider what's required to paint a fresco. First, you have to prepare the surface. You then have to lay plaster, smooth it out, remove imperfections, and wait for it to dry. Once you have your space ready, you then have to produce graphic drawings and build scaffolding that will allow you to reach the ceiling. When Michelangelo got the job from the pope, the first thing he did was put the call out to fellow artists in Florence. Before long, he had fifteen or twenty guys show up in Rome to help him prepare and execute the painting. And it took him—and a staff of twenty—four years to complete the ceiling.

Creativity is a team sport. Those teams that operate the best involve a healthy mix of preexisting and new connections, an ability and willingness to share experiences, and a welcoming of new perspectives.

Hard Work and Mastery

You might have daydreams of success, but what will really get you to achieve them is practice. Showing up each day, putting in the hours and the effort. Repeating the same motion over and over and over until it becomes second nature, whether you're practicing a layup, an incision, or a brushstroke.

Don't shy away from the hard work required for mastery, because skills that you acquire, coupled with the willingness to show up, are the foundation of the creative process. You may not immediately see the connection between the work you are putting in now, the skills you are mastering, and how these enable future creativity, but the link is there. Sometimes, as we work to increase and improve our skills, we are led into different areas and new horizons.

Mastering a skill set is almost always the first step in the creative process. I know it has always been for me—whether in tackling a difficult shoulder replacement, building an inpatient hospital, or making my latest sculpture series.

I don't believe that I've been magically gifted at anything. But I do know that the best things I've done, the best results I've had—whether they have been in surgery, engineering, business, or art—are always the result of hard work. And I firmly believe that doing hard work is a choice.

The Epiphany Myth

I'd like to address a falsehood embedded in our cultural mythology surrounding creativity: the idea that inspiration strikes out of the blue and can't be predicted or repeated. I like to call this the "epiphany myth," since it is born out of the idea of having an epiphany or a eureka moment. Before I start this section, though, I'd like to take a moment to explore what we're left with if we do away with this myth. There has to be something to take its place. If inspiration does not come from a bolt of lightning, where does it come from?

In the introduction, I reviewed a five-stage process for creativity. In chapter 3, I presented it in a linear format since it's easier to understand and apply in this configuration—during preparation, incubation, insight, evaluation, and implementation. Many people think that in order to start something creative, you need to have some sort of "epiphany"—an aha moment of discovery that sets you on a course—and that is all there is to it. But even the epiphany stories we have become familiar with aren't actually "epiphanies" at all.

Let's revisit the famous epiphany story most of us have heard about Isaac Newton, the legendary English mathematician responsible for Newton's law of universal gravitation. As the story goes, he discovered this law when he was sitting in his garden with his back against the trunk of a tree and an apple fell and hit him on the head. And he said to himself, *Whoa, some force must be pulling the apple toward the earth.* And that was the eureka moment, or epiphany. And he then went on and put together Newton's law of universal gravitation.

Another famous epiphany story involves the Greek mathematician Archimedes. Archimedes was asked by his ruler, King Hieron, to evaluate the king's crown. The king had been told the crown was a hundred percent gold and asked Archimedes if he could prove it—without melting it down. Legend has it that Archimedes decided to take a nice, hot bath. He stepped into the bathtub and . . . aha! He was said to have leaped out of the bath saying, "Eureka! Eureka!" which is Greek for "I have found it!" The answer lay in the idea of displacement. He could submerge the crown in water, the amount of displacement would tell him the density, and he could therefore determine whether or not the crown was solid gold.

These are famous, inspirational stories of eureka moments of genius—but these tales contain more than meets the eye. To go back to Newton, he didn't have the epiphany moment at all. A biographer who knew Newton when he was alive said the scientist was in the garden when he saw an apple drop out of a tree. Although it didn't hit him, it did spark Newton's thinking about gravitational forces—thinking that was already quite developed by that point. Newton had already been doing a considerable amount of work on planetary movement and the effects of gravity long before any apple fell out of any tree. And after that moment with the apple, it still took him a number of years to develop a final mathematical explanation for gravity. There were also many steps in Archimedes's process of discovery. He may have taken a bath that prompted him to think of displacement, but he had to learn how to calculate the formula for turning the water displacement measurement into a way to measure density. So there's a lot more to discovery and creativity than just a single epiphanic moment.

So I return to Mihaly Csikszentmihalyi, who in his book *Creativity: Flow and the Psychology of Discovery and Invention* studies the thought processes of ninety-one prominent creative individuals—people like Jonas Salk, the creator of the polio vaccine, and Linus Pauling, a chemist and molecular biologist and two-time Nobel Prize winner, along with many others. What they all had in common is that they let their ideas germinate. In some cases, they put ideas away for a year, and in the meantime they continued to work on other projects or continued with the preparation behaviors and jobs—studying, diving into the subject matter, tending to their skills, and at times taking breaks. Csikszentmihalyi found that Edison did this. Michelangelo did this. Leonardo did this. Darwin did this. When you put an idea away, the unconscious mind is still working away. It is capable of keeping many ideas incubating at the same time right alongside the conscious mind, which is actively working on whatever you have right in front of you in a more immediate way.

As you'll see in the next chapter on incubation, after you've let some ideas lie fallow for a while, insights will begin to arrive. Often, again, it will feel as though these, too, are epiphanies or eureka moments. The penny will drop, and it's as if the entire arcade of your mind awakens to this new idea and all the possibilities that come with it. And it's here that many artists and creatives get caught up in the simplistic concept that the idea came to them all at once, when in fact they had been preparing for and unconsciously mulling over a problem or a piece of art for years and years.

I'll give you an example of how this manifested in something many of us use every day: the Post-it Note. As I've mentioned, I sure use a lot of them. I couldn't have written this book without them. My office is filled with flowcharts created by Post-its. But I would not have this tool if not for a couple of intrepid inventors.

In 1966, a young chemist named Spencer Silver joined the 3M Company. 3M was once a mining company and then it became a chemical company, and by the time Silver joined, it was a big Fortune 500 company that manufactured a broad array of products. After two years working on a number of projects, Silver decided he was going to give a little more attention to one of the company's established product lines: adhesives (a.k.a. sticky things). After five years, he had still only concocted a somewhat inferior adhesive. He asked for input about potential uses for a less sticky adhesive from as many people in the company as possible—whoever would listen. One day, Silver showed his project to a chemical engineer named Art Fry, who didn't have much to say about it. But then Fry came back to work after the weekend with an idea. Fry was in a choir at his church and thought it would be helpful to stick little papers in the book to indicate where certain hymns were, without marking the pages permanently.

Fry and Silver created a prototype for what they called a "semi-permanent bookmarker." People at 3M thought it was a pretty good idea, but no one could see much market demand, so there wasn't a ton of interest in pursuing it as a product. A few weeks later, Fry was reviewing a report on an unrelated project and he read a paragraph that was unclear, a paragraph that he wanted to point out without marking up the report itself. So he took one of these little sticky bookmarkers, wrote the issue on the bookmarker, and stuck it next to the paragraph in the report. All of a sudden, he went from a bookmark to a bookmark that could also serve as a note and a way to communicate.

In 1980, twelve years after Silver first developed what he thought was an inferior adhesive, 3M released Post-it Notes. The rest is history. Silver and Fry spent a lot of time in the preparation stage. They experimented with the formula of the glue. They experimented and tinkered with the manufacturing process. They spent time talking to various colleagues. Then the project incubated. Because it was a side project, they were busy focusing on other projects. During one of these incubation stages, Fry had his first insight and the creative idea reached the next stage: it went from the insight stage to the evaluation stage. The initial product wasn't a home run, because it didn't have much market potential. So then came another incubation period, and finally Fry had his second insight, the idea of writing on the bookmark. This shows how the idea moved from evaluation to implementation. They then changed the world with their product.[7]

We like to hear stories of sudden inspiration, like Newton getting hit with an apple or Archimedes leaping from the bathtub. But as we can see with the Post-it Note, creativity is actually part of a process that requires certain steps. Each step or stage is important to the process and vital to the ultimate product.

And once you have mastered all aspects of your subject matter in the preparation stage, you are ready for the next stage: incubation.

---

7. To read the full story behind 3M's Post-it on the company's website, visit https://www.post-it.com/3M/en_US/post-it/contact-us/about-us/.

CASE STUDY

Preparation in Action: Preparing to Reinvent Healthcare

The purpose of creativity is to make us more fully human—not just to create art for art's sake. Its purpose is to enhance our own and others' humanity. I can think of no other venture that more fully exemplifies this than the formation of my healthcare delivery system, which I will refer to as HCDS. For this reason, I have chosen to use the story of developing HCDS as a case study throughout part 2, so that you can see how the five stages of the creative process work in a continuous (though not necessarily linear) manner.

I founded and led HCDS because it gave me a cause—to change the business model of healthcare delivery so that it was more affordable, more accessible, and higher quality. I was inspired by Gandhi's words: "You must be the change you wish to see in this world." If I wanted to see medicine change, I needed to change the way we did things. I was fortunate enough to have found a cause.

My cause was to solve a complex problem. I believed there had to be a better way to treat patients in the office and in the operating room and to streamline the entire process. Ultimately, I wanted to create the safest and most positive patient experience ever.

Not everyone possesses the talents to be a singer, or a dancer, or a composer. After all, creativity is not for artists alone. One can apply these principles to every profession—even something as seemingly dry as medicine or business. In fact, I would argue that there is nothing dry or uncreative about these professions. As in almost all things we do in life, we must be creative to think through problems and find viable solutions.

JTBD 1: Spot a Need

In 1987, a managed care revolution had started on the West Coast and was making its way across the country. The buzzword was "capitation." Capitation is a way of paying healthcare providers in which they receive a set amount of money to cover the supposedly predictable cost of services. But costs in healthcare are never predictable. Cost structures for hospitals and physicians differ, and patients can have complications or comorbidities that affect outcome and cost. Unfortunately, this involved a shift in risk from healthcare provider to insurer, with the latter receiving even more financial gain. I studied healthcare economics. I also had experience delivering healthcare. There was a problem, but capitation was not the solution.

Spot a Need

The need was to transform complicated healthcare products and services, which were expensive, into ones that were higher in quality, lower in cost, and more accessible to the patients and their families. If charitable support were removed, if the governmental cross-subsidies were removed, and if the constraints on competition were removed, the general hospital business model would collapse.

Strategy for a Solution to the Problem

The strategy was to use emerging technologies and business models (the way the firm operates and creates value) to bring affordability, consistent quality, and accessibility to healthcare. We needed to circumvent a choice between quality and affordability. We needed to deliver both.

I have explained that the problem or challenge was producing healthcare services that were higher in quality, lower in cost, and more easily accessible to patients. I started with a systems thinking (looking at the whole issue) approach. This is how the general hospital "iceberg" looked to me:

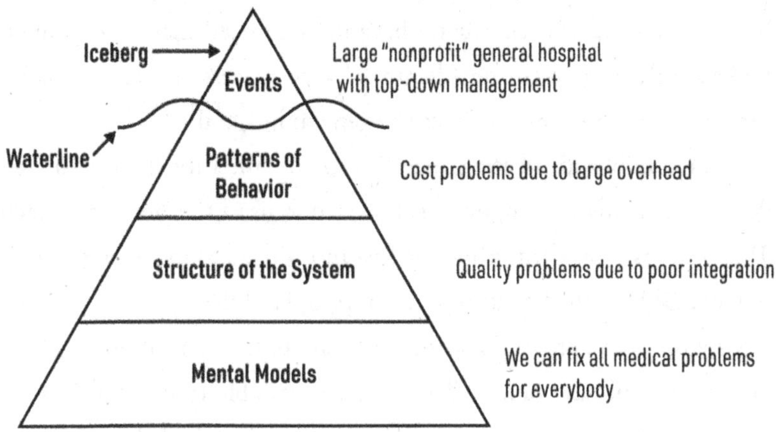

Understanding what "lay below the waterline" was the first step. The goal of the general hospital is to treat everything and everybody. In other words, anybody can show up at the door with any medical condition—the general hospital has to be ready to diagnose and treat the problem. Thousands of different people with thousands of different conditions come through the door each year.

This is a systems nightmare that produces some very unhappy patients—the cost is out of sight and the quality is undependable, to speak nothing of getting lost in a maze of hospital corridors after finally finding parking.

In other words, a general hospital is the equivalent of a factory that is trying to manufacture cars, shoes, pizza, bubble gum, peanut butter, and refrigerators all in the same tower of a building. This is also the direct antithesis of my training as a systems engineer.

Using Systems Thinking to Understand the Problem

As a medical student and later as an orthopedic surgeon, I studied the American healthcare system. I analyzed the different parts of it and how they related to each other. I became convinced that I was going to make a difference in the healthcare delivery process. To do so, I had to zero in on one area, and I chose the general hospital.

The complexity of the general hospital called for it to be broken down into its many components; I needed to use a top-down approach. This systems way of thinking was first introduced to me in engineering school and remained central in developing HCDS.

By the way, applying systems thinking to the general hospital produced a ton of data points. The reason I was able to stay focused was that I lived it every day—on the hospital floors, in the ER, in the operating rooms, and in the clinics. The recurring patterns became quite obvious to me, and they were often dangerous, as I will explain below. But the bottom line was that the cost of healthcare had to come down, quality and safety had to improve, and access had to increase.

Using Design Thinking to Understand the End User's Needs

Idea production took the form of divergent thinking at our brainstorming sessions, but systems and design thinking kept the different departments connected and focused.

Our strategy to drive affordability was to reduce the high overhead costs caused by the complexity of a general hospital.

On the other hand, our strategy to improve quality came from an efficient integration of services around our key customer, the patient.

Yes, you heard me right—we were focusing not on the needs of the hospital and the doctors but on those of the patients and their families.

Whereas systems thinking asks what just happened and what patterns were present, design thinking asks what the customer or user wants and what trends are present.

Thinking Positively When You Fail

Sometimes creativity results in wrong ideas that can cause failures instead of successes. Of course it's a punch in the gut! Of course it sets you back. Of course it's hard to forget. Hearing "Just get over it!" is hardly helpful.

If creative ideas are being produced as part of a systems and design thinking approach, failing is part of a bigger process. *Systems thinkers and design thinkers consider failure to be part of the learning experience.* It's just another step on the road to the experience. Failures will happen. They allow you to figure out what works and what doesn't work. I know it's hard to accept, but the sooner we learn to embrace failure, figure out the next step, and keep going, the easier it will get.

When you are trying to be creative, there will always be those who dare you to be successful and indeed would like to see you collapse. In building HCDS, we had our share of these people—malpractice attorneys, competing "mega" general hospitals, greedy insurance companies, and mindless government agencies, to name a few. What made it all worthwhile were the grateful patients who appreciated that we were trying to be creative caregivers.

Process Creativity over Product Creativity

We found early on at HCDS that if we were going to make a dent in the healthcare universe, process creativity had to trump product creativity.

Especially in orthopedics, new gadgets would be offered by salespeople every day. Sometimes they led to improvements in care, but many times they just increased the complexity. And they were always more costly—ridiculously so.

We discovered that rather than focusing on new products, the best way to improve the patient experience was to arrive at a better understanding of the processes that were part of the systems and design we operated in. Systems and design thinking produced the most effective solution by considering the entire system as well as the patient. In other words, when I thought in terms of the creativity needed in patient care, my goals were always more process oriented than product oriented. The stages of creativity were a process, and creative idea production was a process.

JTBD 2: Acquire Knowledge

Over a twenty-five-year period, I developed a multifield background that was a perfect fit (even though not exactly planned) for acquiring knowledge in healthcare delivery.

I studied systems and industrial engineering and applied it in the aerospace industry. I had been taught how to integrate machines, people, and information efficiently, effectively, and safely to produce goods and services. I studied business at a graduate level and later did a deep dive into healthcare economics. I studied the healthcare delivery and reimbursement models of the United States and several European Union countries. I studied medicine and surgery on both sides of the Atlantic. I had spent years as a resident in orthopedic surgery in Boston before going into private practice.

I understood how general hospitals worked (and didn't work). I worked in the operating rooms, on the hospital floors, and in the clinics. I understood that quality problems were due to poor integration.

In trying to do everything for everybody, most general hospitals had organized their specialist physicians, such as orthopedic surgeons, to stand independently from important supporting services such as physical therapy and MRI. This resulted in complex patient pathways, which resulted in increased overhead costs.

JTBD 3: Gather Information Related to the Problem and Learn from Other Industries

Years after I had ended my formal business training, I continued to read and carry out my research on business model innovation in industries far removed from healthcare delivery. I was aided by the writings of and meetings with Clay Christensen and Michael Porter. At Harvard Business School, I had explained our business model and how I started a separate management company so management would have their own "field" and to exchange ideas with clinicians. It all started because, as a surgeon, I was tired of hearing complaints—from my colleagues and patients alike. Frankly, I had plenty of my own as well.

As an orthopedic surgeon, I was in the clinics and operating rooms five to six days per week. I was one of many clinicians (doctors, nurses, physician's assistants, physical therapists, lab technicians, radiology techs, and so on) who delivered patient care. Since the doctors usually headed up these services, they were often referred to as "the Docs." Meanwhile, a management team was responsible for a regional, vertically integrated healthcare delivery network. This was the business side of HCDS, which included finance, accounting, technology, marketing, and human resources. These employees were referred to as "the Suits."

In healthcare there was a major disconnect between the Docs and the Suits (which remains true in many large systems today). I recognized this throughout my training and when I went into private practice. The Suits and the Docs are trained differently, have different missions, and in general, just think differently. It wasn't just that the offense and defense did not support each other—sometimes they were not even on the same team!

As someone trained in both the clinical and management fields, I could promote the intersection of ideas. Not only could I play offense and defense, but I could act as the team captain that promoted cooperation and the resulting innovation. These industries reinforced the concept that cost problems were often caused by complexity-driven overhead while quality problems were usually due to poor integration. These were lessons that I kept using over and over again as we built a focused regional healthcare delivery network.

Lessons from Worksite Visits

While researching and building my company, I made it a practice to visit countless worksites: steel mills, candy factories, meatpacking plants, crayon factories, trucking depots, and warehouses. This was a practice HCDS associates carried out for decades. Even though those industries are unrelated to healthcare delivery, we learned many lessons in both operations and the customer experience that would be introduced at HCDS. This worksite "look, ask, and learn" approach also allowed HCDS associates to better understand the healthcare needs of the employers and employees and those who were paying the healthcare bill. When I wasn't visualizing, I was drawing, using flowcharts, and taking notes obsessively. All along the way, I was relying on my teams, borrowing ideas from the best, especially during my worksite visits. It was during these visits that I used the creative stage of preparation to solve a problem. The problem was complex: I wanted to reinvent how we treated patients in the office and in the operating room and to streamline the entire process—from where they got treated, how they did, and when they did, to how much they paid for it. I also wanted to create the safest and most positive patient experience ever.

I hoped to make the patient experience more humane. I hoped to bring some humanity to my own profession as well. Ultimately, my hope was to create an aesthetic and healing experience for patients from the moment they left their home until they arrived at one of our facilities. I utilized visualization from the outset. I envisioned patients driving a short distance to the HCDS facility closest to their home. Once they arrived, they would pull their car right up to the facility. Before entering, they would be greeted by beautiful flowers in a serene garden-like scene. There would be no lab sample drop boxes lined up outside the front doors, like you might see at other facilities. The intake process would be smooth and coordinated. Everything would be entered into a software database so a patient wouldn't have to repeatedly provide the same information. Waiting rooms would be well-appointed; the staff would be friendly and knowledgeable. The operating rooms would all have windows with beautiful landscaping outside. All the ORs would be set up in an efficient manner. Patients would be operated on and sent home the same day. They would have shorter wait times, lower infection rates, and overall better outcomes. I visualized it all.

Fortunately, we were able to add "extras" into our patient experience because we managed our overhead differently than the bigger hospitals. For example, we could have plants and landscaping at our facilities and have a better margin on the surgery even though we got paid less than the general hospitals.

Archetype: Learner

For the twenty-five-plus years leading up to the founding of HCDS, the archetype that served me best was the Learner. The attributes of being a Learner—specifically, being open, humble, and brave—helped me dig for the answers to so many questions. I recall a time when I sat at a Bethlehem Steel factory learning about Bessemer furnaces and steel production. Here I learned about exposure to injuries, as well as vertical integration. My commitment to finding the answers, and my patience and grit, steeled my resolve, especially during the tough times.

More a Cause Than a Mission

When you have a cause, the story you tell about it is a forever-changing narrative. Having a cause means taking risks and making some big blunders, but being creative and feeling fully alive. The plot can change. In fact, there are multiple plots to my life story. As I mention in this book, there have been several times in my life when I have said to myself, *Emilio, you need a new story.* At these times, I was fortunate to be able to construct another narrative. Having a cause means taking the time to ask what kind of person you really want to be. In hunting for this answer, I came to understand the meaning of being fully human and fully alive. Having a cause means digging deep to determine what type of work brings out the real you. Having a cause means taking the time to ask yourself, *Why is this work important to me?* This is a question I had to ask, once again, before deciding to write this book. When I finally answered this question, I realized there were several sides to me. I was fortunate to live as a multifield creative. I believe that the "intersection" of fields (systems, medicine, sculpture) allowed me, as an individual, to be more innovative in the business of healthcare delivery—to have a cause.

According to a 2017 research study conducted by Jing Hu and Jacob Hirsh at the University of Toronto, when workers consider a job meaningful—that is, when they have a cause—they are willing to choose lower salaries.[8] I can relate to this; my decision to leave Grumman and graduate school in 1972 at first appeared to be a step backward. In fact, it changed my life. Putting purpose and cause ahead of money has given me a more creative life, a life that has allowed me to feel more fully human.

Many millennials and members of Gen Z have other ideas when it comes to career fulfillment too. These people, who constitute nearly 50 percent of the workforce, are rethinking their careers. In many cases, they are leaving their jobs. They are walking away from assigned missions (the American dream of working hard, earning more, having more, and maybe even being well known) and looking instead for chosen causes. In a 2023 survey, nearly three-quarters of Gen Z and millennials said they were thinking of a job change.[9]

Even the current state of the economy will not deter them. Even if they receive less compensation or recognition, they are looking for work-life balance and a purpose or cause to show up for each day. I think what they are really saying is that they want to feel fully alive, fully human. They want to embrace creativity in their work and in their lives. This is a major difference from my postcollege years, when many chose profit over purpose.

Of course, many of us have to make choices that serve our needs at a particular point in our lives. I know that was the case for me. But the point is that the story doesn't have to stop there. I studied engineering and business to make sure I could support myself. But I had to draw and paint to stay human. I became an orthopedic surgeon

---

8. Jing Hu and Jacob B. Hirsh, "Accepting Lower Salaries for Meaningful Work," *Frontiers in Psychology* 8 (2017): Article 1649, https://doi.org/10.3389/fpsyg.2017.01649.

9. Morgan Smith, "70% of Gen Z and Millennials Are Considering Leaving Their Jobs Soon," CNBC, January 18, 2023, https://www.cnbc.com/2023/01/18/70percent-of-gen-z-and-millennials-are-considering-leaving-their-jobs-soon.htm.

because it brought me closer to the human condition and gave me a greater purpose.

I applied hard work and the mastery of my subject matter to all aspects of the preparation stage. And after years and years of this preparation, I was ready for the next stage: incubation.

Jump-Start Your Creativity

Writing prompts for your journal:

- What creative activity are you currently in the preparation stage for? If you aren't already preparing, what challenge are you facing that you need to address?
- Are you currently reading or learning everything you can about this challenge?
- Do you have a deliberate practice?
- What creative actions or behaviors do you find most helpful? Do you find that you get your creative juices flowing by visualizing, drawing, or team-building? Are there any other behaviors I have not mentioned that serve you well and that you can incorporate into the preparation stage to make it your own?
- In what ways can you apply creativity to the field you currently work in? If you do not consider yourself an "artist," how do you stay creative?
- What fields outside your work could you consider "combining" or working with? Think about what other fields of expertise could help you approach your problem in a new way.
- Do you have a "cause" or a "purpose," or is your work simply task oriented (mission based)? Is there something that fuels you or makes you want to get up and go? What drives you? That might be your cause and purpose!

CHAPTER 5

Stage 2: Incubation

Let Your Higher Subconscious Work on the Resolution to the Problem

I have found that ideas and their connections have to germinate. They cannot be forced. They must be allowed to unfold like the blooming of a lotus flower. And just as the lotus blooms only after the stalk emerges from its roots in the murky depths, out of sight of the naked eye, the layers of nuance needed to solve a problem unfurl only after ideas have had time to develop in the depths of the subconscious mind. In order to give your mind time to process all the information it has learned and acquired during the preparation stage, this information needs to incubate. The incubation stage is a subconscious process of idea selection and combination.

I liken this stage to making my all-important cup of coffee in the morning. When my coffee percolates, water is filtered through the porous, though flavorful, layers of ground coffee beans. When our pot heats up, the water is taken up by the tube, and then it trickles over the coffee through the filter. You simply let the hot water percolate and filter through the beans, nothing more, nothing less. Everything you have and need is encased in the beans. You simply need to surrender and trust the process and trust that while you are waiting everything is working out. Similarly, we human "beans" are made up of many layers of life experiences. Some new. Some old. Some very old. When we are at rest, the necessary ideas percolate like water in the coffee maker—they come up from the subconscious, they combine with our experiences and knowledge, and all of these commingle to produce a seemingly magical result. These ideas will be revealed to you in conscious thought later in the process—at the insight stage—but for now, you must trust that the unconscious process of percolation never stops. The coffee beans don't have to do anything. They sit in the filter—at rest—as the water flows through them, creating the new flavor. Similarly, the conscious mind rests during the incubation stage, and the unconscious mind, like the water, is busy allowing disparate ideas to simmer and come together. Albert Einstein coined the term "combinatory play" to describe what happens when the subconscious is activated while the conscious mind is at rest or "playing." It is well known that he often played the violin when working through difficult problems. He put the problems aside and let his brain rest; it was then, while playing the violin, that his ideas and experiences combined.

Long before Albert Einstein coined the term "combinatory play," many other great minds and thinkers were doing it. In Christian Meier's biography of Julius Caesar, *Caesar*, Meir describes how Caesar wrote poetry for recreation as a break from planning his escape from the pirates who had kidnapped him. Later, in 46 BC, during the Great

Roman Civil War, the last of Pompey's army was encamped in Spain. Caesar sailed to Spain to prepare for the final and decisive battle of the civil war. Onboard his ship, before he arrived in Spain, he wrote a poem called *Iter* (The Journey). Again, in the midst of one of the greatest problems he had yet to solve, the threat of his country's fall, he stopped and wrote poetry. I believe it was the incubation period he needed to gear up and strategize for the Battle of Munda.

Another creative mind who utilized incubation was the impressionist painter Claude Monet. In 1883, Monet bought a property in a small rural town an hour outside Paris called Giverny. He needed a property big enough for his large family, which consisted of his own two children and, after his first wife died of cancer, his new wife and her six children. He fell in love with a house and garden that he rented and later bought in 1890. Giverny turned out to be Monet's primary inspiration for the last three decades of his life. He created a Japanese garden for contemplation and relaxation. He dug out a pond and filled it with water lilies and an arched bridge. Monet believed that his garden at Giverny was his "most beautiful masterpiece" and observed, "I perhaps owe having become a painter to flowers."[1] When he wasn't planting, he walked in his gardens. This provided him with hours of time to incubate ideas. Ideas of shape and form, but above all color. And while he found respite in the garden at Giverny, he also found his ultimate success as an artist—his water lily paintings. He could not have created the water lily paintings had he not toiled away in the garden—away from his canvas and paints. He, too, put his paintbrush down and spent time playing in another arena—his garden, which ultimately informed his work.

---

1. "Nature's Palette: 10 Inspiring Quotes by Claude Monet," Beyond Monet: The Immersive Experience, accessed December 8, 2025, https://beyondmonet.com/10-inspiring-quotes-by-claude-monet/.

But it is not just scientists, statespeople, and artists who benefit from incubation. Back in 1971, a friend of mine from New York, Jan, was telling me over a glass of wine how much she loved working as an executive assistant for John Reed, a young MIT grad at Citicorp. She told me that besides being a great boss and teacher, John was one of the most creative people she had ever met. You may be thinking what most would when they heard that he was a banker: *A creative banker? Really?* Jan proceeded to tell me about John's curious methodology. At just thirty-one years old, he often escaped to the beach for a few days after intense days at the office. He would walk alone or sit on the beach and then later, in a quiet hotel room, he would scribble in a notebook. She told me how one day he came back from the beach with an idea for a money-dispensing machine. Yes, while sitting on the beach, not in his office, the idea of the street-level bank automated teller machine (ATM) came to him. Within nine years, ATMs were all over New York, and by the nineties, they were ubiquitous. John Reed rose to become chair and chief executive of Citicorp (later Citigroup), and during his tenure he took many beach trips and reconsidered the business model of consumer banking.

JTBD 1: Lose Control and Trust the Process

What all these stories show is that by taking a break from thinking about the problem, you put aside the hard work of preparation and you let your mind rest. You can't force incubation—it will not work very well if you have a deadline. You need to take your time and trust that ideas will germinate.

Researchers have shown that incubation works by tapping into your subconscious after you've done the hard work required in the preparation stage. The difference is that the preparation stage is a conscious stage you can control, while the incubation stage is subconscious and thus uncontrollable.

I have never been one to churn out ideas on cue. It takes me time. I learned over the years to trust my subconscious and the process. I believe that the most important game plan for thinking (and acting!) creatively is to think in a receptive way. To maximize the unconscious process, information needs to be mapped out in an impartial manner. You must have a wide-open mindset for new ideas and experiences. I have often found it beneficial to separate from the immediate work at hand and give myself time to consider other points of view. When I return, the ideas are clearer—for better or worse. Allowing my present attempts at creative ideas to go subconscious—that is, into imagination mode—is not always easy. But it has gotten simpler as the decades of past experiences have made "combinatory play" more efficient.

I have learned that I need a pause, an interval, between creative endeavors. Over the years, my ability to relax and trust that my subconscious imagination will produce the right ideas and solutions has been fostered by my multiple creative identities and my work in systems, surgery, and sculpture, or what I call the three S's. The three S's allow me to turn on one of these switches, while turning the other two off.

And none of us are too busy or too bogged down by the weight of the world to take time off. Even Winston Churchill, the man behind the oft-quoted "Never give in, never give in, never, never, never, never—in nothing, great or small, large or petty," gave in and took a day off as a statesperson and leader. In fact, prior to becoming the prime minister, Winston Churchill was out of office and remained so for nearly ten years, or what are now called his "wilderness years." During this time, though he wasn't working or active in an office, his ideas were percolating and he was the lone voice against the appeasement of the tidal wave of fascism crashing through Europe. While Hitler rose in Germany and Nazism spread, Churchill was on his estate in Chartwell, digging fishponds and laying bricks, repairing slate roofs, and writing articles and books. By the time he became prime minister at the opening of

World War II, he was ready to fight fascism and had the reserves, mentally and physically, to truly "never, never, never give in." His intuition, instincts, strategies, and sense of calm were unmatched against any enemy, and that was in large part, I believe, because of the connections he made during his incubation stage.

JTBD 2: Allow Connections to Be Made During Subconscious Work

I can only assume based on the outcome that even when Churchill wasn't "working" on solving fascism and was laying brick, his mind was working on the problem below the level of consciousness. This subconscious work results in better solutions because it allows the brain to make new connections between previously unrelated concepts. When one goes back to consciously generating solutions, these connections are more readily available, enabling people to generate more unusual solutions.

Visual artist Milton Glaser, the world-famous graphic designer behind the "I ♥ NY" logo, relied on this process: "The creative process is essentially a blind process, where you do not pre-structure and you have to allow information to arise in a spontaneous way, uncontrollable by the will . . ."[2]

And there is a scientific basis for this. When we turn off the focusing part of our brain, we activate something called the default mode network (DMN)—or the "do mostly nothing" mode—as opposed to the cognitive control network (CCN), which turns on when we focus and try to solve a problem. For a long time, scientists took this literally—that when we weren't thinking, the brain was at rest and "nothing" was really happening. Thanks to the beauty of science and functional

2. Matt Rud, "Mad Men design heroes—Milton Glaser," Myfonts.com, https://www.myfonts.com/a/font/content/mad-men-design-heroes-milton-glaser.

magnetic resonance imaging (fMRI), we now know this network uses more energy than any other network in the brain, consuming roughly 20 percent of the body's energy *while at rest.*

Functional MRI doesn't only measure how much energy we use; it also measures and maps the brain's activity. It can track small changes in blood flow that occur with brain activity. By showing the blood flow, it indicates which parts of the brain are being stimulated. Functional brain imaging shows that different parts of the brain are active during creative problem-solving. The CCN of the brain is active when people are consciously focused on solving a problem, and when the CCN is not working, another system spontaneously kicks in—the DMN.

For a little perspective, any kind of effort on our part requires just 5 percent more energy than is required in the DMN. This is all to say that the DMN is doing anything but "nothing" or "resting" and operates completely under our conscious radar—it works in our subconscious. When we turn our "focus" brain off, our brain has the capacity and energy to retrieve autobiographical memories and experiences and link ideas (to combine, to percolate, to make the proverbial coffee). It also helps interpretate new stimuli based on previous knowledge. And it helps guide future behavior by using previous experiences. Interestingly, this period of rest also allows us to feel more connected to ourselves and gain insights and understanding about ourselves, which in turn help us gain insights into the minds of others. You're more likely to think clearly and even predict things more accurately. The higher the fMRI activity in the DMN, the higher the level of creativity.

Activities That Assist and Activate the DMN

What Mozart didn't know was that when he was doing these things, he was activating his DMN. The following activities can help you activate your DMN.

Daydreaming, Imagining, and Mind Wandering

Most of us can recall a time when we were called upon in a class, a lecture, or an office meeting and we were "not there." Our mind was elsewhere—perhaps staring out the window at a leaf falling from a tree, imagining our upcoming vacation, or thinking about walking through the door at home at the end of the day. While often looked down upon in schools and the working world, daydreaming, imagining, and mind wandering are essential to the creative mind. In many areas of modern society, this concept of letting the mind wander is foreign. We are expected to "do stuff" or "get it done" at all times. But your mind needs a chance to relax. Your mind needs a chance to wander. Albert Einstein famously said, "Logic will take you from A to B. Imagination will take you everywhere."

Multitasking

On a different note, researchers like Keith Sawyer, author of *Explaining Creativity*, have also shown that some creative people multitask in "networks of enterprise." They make sure they're working on more than one project at the same time. While they're consciously attending to one project, the others are incubating. For them, the unconscious mind seems to be able to incubate on many projects at once "in parallel," unlike the conscious mind, which can focus on only one thing at a time.[3] I have always found that my imagination is enhanced when I am multitasking. For instance, at the present time, while working on

---

3. This is my paraphrase of Keith Sawyer's interpretation of Howard Gruber's "networks of enterprise" theory, and it appears in Sawyer's book *Explaining Creativity: The Science of Human Innovation*, 2nd ed. (Oxford University Press, 2012), specifically in chapter 4, which addresses the cognitive mechanisms behind multitasking in creative work.

ceramic sculptures, I have also begun a new series of black, monochromatic paintings. In this manner, my conscious and my subconscious can dance together. We all know that multitasking has gotten a bad name. Trying to do more than one thing at a time is said to reduce performance. But for me, multitasking actually increases my mental activity and thus increases creativity. Multitasking demands that I pay attention to the task at hand while prompting my memory. In other words, if our brains can achieve a higher level of activation, they can use that energy in different ways to make us more creative.

When managing my healthcare delivery system or working as a surgeon, I would multitask between healthcare delivery and painting or sculpture. Another entrepreneur who did much the same was Alexander Liberman. Liberman was the editorial director and deputy chair of all Condé Nast publications, such as *Vogue* and *Traveler*. During this time, he was also a prolific painter, sculptor, photographer, and writer. According to the biography *Alex*, by Dodie Kazanjian and Calvin Tomkins, he painted on the weekends and this was his "spiritual anchor," just as important to him as his career at Condé Nast.[4] One could argue that his creative vision at Condé Nast was informed by his own art and that his art was inspired by the work he did during the week at Condé Nast.

Sleeping

While deep sleep is considered the most essential, REM sleep assists in salvaging forgotten memories. Never underestimate the power of a midday nap or a good night's sleep to rejuvenate you. A tired President Abraham Lincoln boarded a train in Washington, DC, on November

---

4. Dodie Kazanjian and Calvin Tomkins, *Alex: The Life of Alexander Liberman* (Alfred A. Knopf, 1993), 209.

18, 1863, on his way to give a speech in Pennsylvania. He had written five drafts and was painstakingly considering each word for days leading up to the trip. Instead of rewriting on the train, he took a nap. That evening he stayed at the home of David Wills, and again after some rest put the finishing touches on the short speech about ideals worth dying for—what became the Gettysburg Address.

Taking a Break

Another way to walk away from the preparatory stage is literally walking. Take a long walk, go shopping, step out of your routine and regular workspaces, and try something new. Attend a free concert in the park, a traveling art exhibition at a local gallery or museum, or visit a local historic site or garden center. If you can afford to, book a small vacation. You don't need to get away for long; any break from the ordinary or your routine is beneficial. Travel breaks up your "focus" on what is going on at work—as long as you leave your laptop behind and refrain from filling your head with future emails you want to send when you return to your desk. If you allow it to, travel exposes you to new sounds, sights, and sensations. Immersing yourself in a new culture increases your mind's ability to move between different ideas, think more deeply, and integrate thoughts.

Trying New Things

If travel isn't in your budget or you have responsibilities at home that make frequent getaways impossible, you can do things at home that give your brain a mini vacation. You can explore a new part of town, stroll through a park, or visit a bookstore or antique shop. You can take a cooking or pottery class offered in your community. No matter your budget, there are always ways to find mini escapes from your routine.

Julia Cameron, in her book *The Artist's Way*, recommends what she calls "artist dates." You don't need to spend money; you just need to step out of your studio or office and into the world and expose yourself to something completely new and different—perhaps visit a local museum or gallery, listen to some live music at a coffeehouse, or walk aimlessly through a thrift store.

Reading for Enjoyment (Not Research)

One of the best ways to escape from your research and preparation is reading for pleasure—novels, memoirs, nonfiction, poetry, or material on any topic not related to the one you are researching. Lin-Manuel Miranda, the Tony Award–winning writer and creator of Broadway sensation *In the Heights*, was exhausted from his run on Broadway. Taking a break, he went on vacation and began reading a Ron Chernow biography of US Revolutionary War hero and founding father Alexander Hamilton. Miranda's father, a political adviser, had recommended he read the book on vacation to take his mind off Broadway. And what could be less Broadway than the Revolutionary War? But something took hold of Miranda as he read about this unlikely subject of a future Broadway play. He thought, at most, he would write a song about the duel between Hamilton and his rival Aaron Burr, but before he knew it, he had created a new musical—which would become the worldwide phenomenon that is *Hamilton*.

Enjoying Nature

For years there have been reams of anecdotal evidence linking the impact of nature on creativity. Painters like Georgia O'Keeffe drew on nature as a source of ideas through incubation. Poets like William Wordsworth repeatedly emphasized the importance of nature to an individual's creativity, from both intellectual and spiritual senses. Recently the *Journal of Environmental Psychology* published an article on the scientific basis for this link between nature and the incubation stage of creativity, citing an increased capacity for creative endeavors with exposure to nature.[5] But we don't need science to confirm what most of us know—we feel better after spending time in nature, taking advantage of whatever natural resources we have at our disposal. If you live by the ocean, you can walk by the sea, soak up the sea air, go into the water and swim, or sit on the shore and watch the waves crash as the sun rises or sets. Take a long walk and let your mind wander. If you live by the mountains or forest—go on a hike. Live in a city? Find a local park or a community garden, or nurture potted plants in your apartment or studio. Wherever you are, get outside each day. Your mind and creativity will thank you.

Cultivating Mindfulness and Meditating

One extremely efficient way to heighten your general awareness and mindfulness is through meditation. Most people think meditation means emptying your mind of thoughts or sitting uncomfortably on the floor while chanting "om." While these types of meditation slow down your body and mind so you can tap into the present moment, they don't necessarily make you more aware or mindful. Nevertheless, it's a place to start. So often in our everyday lives, our minds are inundated with noise, digital devices, visual stimuli, and overall agitation. Escaping this overloaded switchboard for a frame of mind of silence and undivided attention can be hugely beneficial to the creative process.

---

5. Eleanor Ratcliffe, Birgitta Gatersleben, Paul T. Sowden, and Kalevi M. Korpela, "Understanding the Perceived Benefits of Nature for Creativity," *Journal of Environmental Psychology* 63 (2019): 1–11.

One type of meditation that can help the creative process is "insight meditation." This is different from breathwork—counting and manipulating inhales and exhales—which can relax or activate the sympathetic nervous system in your body. Instead, insight meditation offers just what it says—insight into your thoughts and mind. When you practice insight meditation, you are noticing and allowing, but not attaching to, all the thoughts, feelings, ideas, and insights that come to your mind. You witness the thought and then you let it go. This ultimately brings about awareness and wisdom. You soon realize that you aren't your thoughts. They don't run the show. Rather, you are the observer of these thoughts and ideas, and you're watching them pass through your mind like clouds in the sky or a leaf floating downstream. You can take or leave these thoughts, feelings, and sensations as they arise. Over time, with practice, you become much more aware of your mind and how it works. Soon this carries over into every aspect of your life. You can almost "detach from" and "observe" the world around you and the actions you and others are taking. You can recognize emotions, whims, and desires—and can respond mindfully to them. By becoming more conscious and mindful of the world around you, you reach an active state of heightened observation. Soon you start to see the new, the unusual, or the things you never noticed before. You may be on a walk and notice that the curvature of a tree branch looks like the sway of a woman's hip, or you may notice the beautiful hands of the server pouring your coffee in the restaurant. You might notice the ergonomic nature of your chair or a streamlined process being orchestrated in the kitchen. You may hear the chirping of birds that sounds like a melody you'd like to explore. As you walk along a windswept beach and hear the crash of the waves and rumble of the rocks in the undertow, you may hear the bass line in a composition that has eluded you. Or you might see an image of a family playing by the beach that would be perfect for your next ad campaign. By slowing down and becoming more mindful of not just our thoughts, feelings, and perceptions but the world around us, we can tap into untold reserves of creative power everywhere.

The Incubation Archetype: Voyager

The archetype for the incubation stage is the Voyager. The Voyager is able to navigate uncharted territory and find their own way, remaining open to exploring all kinds of ideas and concepts. They aren't tethered to one place, idea, or concept. They have the ability to surrender, be flexible, and feel appreciation.

Surrender

One of the most difficult things in life is letting go of control and allowing things to unfold. Because we are naturally wired for self-protection, humans like to know where the next threat is coming from. One of the ways we think we can protect ourselves is by controlling our environments and, sometimes, other people and circumstances. Buddhists and philosophers understand that this need to control leads to attachment (to outcomes) and therefore suffering. Almost all suffering is created by some form of attachment—we are by nature attached to our loved ones, our family, our children, our pets, our work, our careers, our homes, our worldviews. To lose any one of those things, or to experience just the threat of losing one, causes us to suffer. So much of the pain and angst we feel in our work as creatives results from wanting things to occur in the here and now. We want certain results, in a certain time frame, in a certain way. We want the answer to the problem yesterday, not tomorrow. The opposite of control is surrender—letting go of the outcome. Allowing is like flowing with the current. Controlling is paddling upstream. I often let my intuition, subconscious, and years of experiences take over in my art studio. In order to do so, I have to let go of control. Voyagers allow and don't try to control. They remain carefree and relaxed in the moment—they are open to receive any experience on their journey. They stop trying to be perfect. They often spend time doing nothing. They don't take themselves too seriously and aren't worried about what others think. They surrender to the flow of activity—like a child playing in the sandbox or on the swings. They simply are there to enjoy themselves, nothing more, nothing less.

Be Flexible

Voyagers are unattached to concrete belief systems, concepts, and itineraries; they are open to experiences and are highly adaptive. If someone invites them on a walk, they go. If the need for a nap overwhelms them, they take it. They are able to unplug and step away from work. In the preparation stage, the Learner fills their mind as much as they can. They push their mind to the limits. In incubation, there is no pushing. In yoga, there is the yin and the yang. The yang focuses on building strength, balance, and alignment. The yin focuses on stretching, resting, allowing, and grounding—so one can stay flexible, not just strong. During the yin practice of Savasana after a long yang practice, your body rests prostrate on a mat, while your mind and body form the connection it made during practice. Think of incubation as the Savasana for the mind. Your mind empties, but it is still working. In doing so, the mind produces the capacity, or room, for the answers or ideas to develop and occur.

Appreciate

Voyagers have an innate appreciation and love for the beauty around them. They can enjoy their surroundings without needing to own them. They express gratitude and allow themselves to be overcome with awe and wonder by their surroundings, marveling at whatever seems to stimulate. When you show appreciation, you prime your brain to look for things to be inspired or awed by. The more you appreciate, the more you find to appreciate. Appreciation opens up pathways in the brain to receive more. If you're feeling stuck, or tired, or overworked, stop what you're doing and write a thank-you letter of appreciation or list things for which you are grateful. The very act will not only inspire you but may inspire others.

The Myth of Productivity

One of the biggest myths is that in order to produce creative output, you must constantly be busy. Hustle culture is alive and well. But it's important to remember that productivity is not the same as creativity. Taking a step away is essential to the process.

Most of the fruits of incubation will not reveal themselves until the insight stage. It is easy to be frustrated or feel stuck when you're incubating. In fact, you may even be met with resistance from those around you. You may hear from well-meaning friends and colleagues, "Why aren't you working? Isn't there something you could be doing?" It's easy to fall victim to the notion that one must always be doing something in order to see great results. While we're incubating, to outsiders it doesn't look like much is happening. It may not look that way to them, but we know work is happening. In his best-selling book *Greenlights*, Matthew McConaughey tells the story of how when he first made it to Hollywood, he was working it. He was trying to get auditions and looking for agents, but things weren't lining up. On a whim, he and his buddies decided to motorcycle through Europe together. He was young and had no responsibilities, so he went for it. He just had fun, allowing things to unfold. Shortly after he came back, he was cast in a role. He had to be patient and trust that things would work out in Hollywood. And it's safe to say, after starring in a number of blockbuster hits and winning the Oscar for Best Actor, McConaughey did "alright, alright, alright."

Some of the most fertile parts of the creative process happen when seemingly nothing is happening. Allow nothing to happen, knowing that everything is falling into place. Any sommelier knows that some of the best wines are those that have time to sit in the bottle, where the flavors and notes can commingle. Allow your brain to rest, and let your memories, knowledge, and intuition work together to provide the insights you need to create.

When the next three conscious stages (insight, evaluation, and implementation) take over, these connections will have been made and will be available. This means the ability to produce more and better solutions will be enhanced. For me, incubation and imagination are synonymous. As psychologist Carl Jung, who studied the subconscious, said, "The debt we owe to the play of imagination is incalculable." And you will see the payoff in the next stage—insight.

CASE STUDY

Incubation in Action: Incubating New Solutions

In developing a healthcare delivery system that was safer, cheaper, and more accessible, there were many challenges. Because these challenges varied in scope and complexity, the incubation stages for each challenge varied in duration. Sometimes they were brief (minutes to hours). Sometimes they were moderate (days to weeks). The longer incubation periods could take much longer (months to years).

The longer incubation periods usually performed a nonlinear dance with the preparation stage and bounced back and forth. These longer incubation periods had to take into account dynamic changes in areas such as arthroscopic surgery, spine surgery, joint replacement, and diagnostic imaging.

These longer incubation periods also had to take into account changes in the political environment that resulted in abrupt changes in payment reimbursements. But regardless of the complexity of the problem and the period of incubation, the process was the same. During the preparation stage, my team and I consciously formed new ideas for possible solutions. To refine these ideas, the incubation stage asked us to push the task out of our immediate attention and hand it off to our subconscious. Our subconscious then began a type of synthesizing process; the new ideas from the preparation stage assimilated with older ideas, experiences, and memories.

As I said, this process can take minutes, weeks, or even years to work through.

Letting the Subconscious Take the Reins and Enhancing the Ability to Dream

I needed to take a step back from actively thinking about the problem and give my ideas space before launching back in. What follows are some concepts that helped me facilitate these HCDS incubation periods, which, as you will see, were not always as simple as mind wandering and daydreaming.

Playing in the Fireman's Hat

I remember as a child escaping into my mystical worlds. I did this with the aid of drawing. I once created an entire community that lived in a fireman's hat. Somehow, this magical hat with its large crown, visor, and sloping rear rim had many projects and people humming about within it. I can't quite explain it, but I believe there was a connection between my childhood ability to live in this fantasy world of a fireman's hat and my later creative success as an adult.

Here is where the visualization process once again comes in. Before opening HCDS, I would often daydream about what the ideal OR would look like, how the perfect communication between surgeon and therapist would work, how a direct linkage between radiologist and surgeon could be developed, and so on. Eventually, I would daydream about what a regional healthcare delivery network might look like.

I would put on my "imagineering hat" and travel into the future, dreaming of new business models that would provide for the ultimate patient experience. This daydreaming occurred as I walked down general hospital corridors, as I left an operating room, or when I walked into the cornfield that would be the site of our first ORs. In the early HCDS days, I remember daydreaming in a diner and sketching on a napkin what would result in HCDS's first sports medicine clinic.

But even at this early time at HCDS, it was about the intersection of fields.

The design of our clinic was created at the intersection of personalities one night at a Greek diner, when I sat down with Manny, a gregarious guy with a big smile and a can-do attitude. He was born in a small Greek village and somehow found his way to study architecture at the Sorbonne in Paris. He wore his black hair at shoulder level and wore jeans and sneakers. He wanted to build innovative buildings, and we teamed up. After an incubation period of about six months, we broke ground for the first of a series of regional clinics that changed access and treatment for the injured athlete.

Walking Away—but Then What?

I often needed to walk away from the preparation stage and let it go. But what was I going to do when I let it go? I needed to do something that engaged me mentally and physically and was different from the HCDS preparatory stage. I walked into an operating room and focused on the surgery in front of me. When I left the operating room, I had an art studio at home I loved equally. The conscious activities of surgery, clinics, painting, and sculpture allowed me to leave the business models in my subconscious.

Trying Completely New Things

Another method of pushing the immediate challenges of healthcare delivery out of the conscious mental zone and into the incubation of the unconscious was trying completely new things.

Starting a Diverse Home Library

My bedtime reading turned to American and European history. I read about Franklin, Jefferson (I studied the architecture of Monticello), Adams, and the Roosevelts. On the European side, I dove into Caesar, Napoleon, and Churchill, especially his estate at Chartwell.

It was at this time that I began more seriously to grow my at-home library. Amazon came into my life, and I could not only easily obtain a book on the twelve Caesars but start an art book collection that continues to grow to this day. My bookshelves became a wonderful way to give my HCDS ideas space before I launched back in. By reading something unconnected to the field I was working in, I opened my mind to all kinds of new perspectives and ideas. I recall finishing the last pages of a book on Julius Caesar and putting it down and feeling truly inspired. He was at his best bringing together people from different fields, incubating ideas but executing to produce incredible innovations that we still use today. Unfortunately, it was a bit too much for the Roman Senate and they killed him.

It was late in the history of HCDS that I would dive into the world of social science.

I needed to better understand the career experiences I'd had, especially in founding and leading HCDS. I did a deep dive into positive psychology, and in particular creativity.

I had a whole new set of teachers, including Graham Wallas, Mihaly Csikszentmihalyi, and Keith Sawyer. My library had a new division devoted to books in the creativity and innovation space.

From this research and my own experiences, I decided to tell the creativity story as I saw it. Hence this book you are reading.

Talking to the Trees

Walking through the woods, communicating with the trees, catching a glimpse of a doe and her new fawn, and experiencing the changing seasons is something spiritual for me. It is as mystical as the incubation process itself. I didn't know for sure that in these moments ideas were being linked that would help me figure out how to finance that new hospital HCDS was building. But I had to trust. Just like you are not quite sure the tall trees are listening, but you're going to talk to them anyway.

Once again, I believe that idea quality is enhanced by the "intersection." We have seen that the intersection of ideas can occur within an individual or team. But it can also occur when cultures intersect—the woodland culture of Thoreau and the complex culture of modern management science.

Meditation

As HCDS grew, we were managing twelve thousand patient encounters per week while striving for innovative creativity. Many times, I needed a shorter incubation period. I found that during the short incubation period, meditation had an important role.

Focusing my mind on my breathing for twenty minutes at a time allowed me to temporarily unwind, push the challenges out of my mind, and reach an almost spiritual awareness.

While I was a physician, I found time in the middle of the day for short but effective meditation periods during my lunch. I used to sit in my ten-year-old Sequoia in the busy parking lot of the outpatient clinic, eat my apple slices smeared with peanut butter, and drink a bottle of water. After eating, I'd recline the seat as far back as I could, reach for my eye mask, and start my measured breathing. I knew that in fifteen to twenty minutes I could walk into that clinic and see patients in a more human manner. It was a far cry from the two-martini lunches on Wall Street that I'd escaped from twenty-five years ago. I was happy.

The striving to bring my mental processes under more voluntary control produced a sense of calm, clarity, and concentration. This stable feeling allowed me to better train the attention of my mind.

Summary: Better Solutions Through Intersection of Fields

Because of its complexity, HCDS is a classic example of the nonlinear nature of the creative process. There was a constant need to revisit the preparation stage for further study and idea initiation before returning to the incubation stage and assimilating from the past.

This could take minutes, days, months, or years.

As I said before, HCDS was thirty years in the making. It was a waiting game that demanded that patience underpinned my behavior.

Fortunately, patience was instilled in me as part of my surgical training. Surgeons aren't born—they're made, and it takes time. As I applied the five stages of creativity at HCDS, I realized the importance and the mystery of Stage 2.

Incubation is this dance between the conscious and unconscious. HCDS allowed me a platform for producing ideas and then bringing them to life—a magical balance between imagination and production. Controlling this balance was important for me as an individual.

Ideas for solutions to problems first start in the conscious preparation phase. And during the unconscious phase, the brain *continues* to try to produce ideas for solutions to solve the problem. Research has shown that better solutions often come from this unconscious phase. Why? The brain can more easily make new connections between earlier unrelated ideas, especially if they are coming from different fields. And this is incredibly important in order to gain insights.

Jump-Start Your Creativity

Writing prompts for your journal:

- What creative idea (or ideas) are you currently incubating?
- What switches can you flip to allow your subconscious imagination to flow?
- Are you allowing ample time for rest or are you grinding and hustling, hoping to force a solution? What can you change to allow for more time for incubation?
- What can you do today to step back and let your subconscious do what it needs to do? Take a nap? Take a day off? Try something new?
- What sustains you during periods of incubation?
- What activities are you allowing or actively pursuing so that your mind can rest and incubate a solution to a problem? Where do you feel most energized and present?
- How can you show more appreciation and gratitude in your day? For whom or for what experiences are you most grateful?
- In what ways can you be more flexible? In what areas can you let go of control and surrender a bit more?

CHAPTER 6

Stage 3: Insight

The hard thinking for producing ideas started in the preparation stage (chapter 4) and transitioned to the subconscious cognitive work of finding combinations in chapter 5 (incubation). In this chapter we are back to consciously producing many ideas and their combinations. We call this stage "insight" because we are generating insightful ideas. In other words, we are coming up with problem-solving ideas that are especially perceptive and thought-provoking. We then go on to develop a problem-solving strategy for applying these insightful ideas.

The Only Job to Be Done: Allowing Multiple Ideas to Surface

We have covered preparation and incubation. Both these stages require several Jobs to Be Done. But insight doesn't require several jobs. In some ways this makes insight seem "easier," but it's not. In fact, it's much more complex than the previous two stages. In preparation you were gathering and acquiring, and in incubation you were letting things "happen" by letting your mind wander, letting go of control, and allowing your subconscious to form connections.

When I first set out to write this book, I had originally broken this insight chapter down into several Jobs to Be Done. At the time, I was trying to make everything fit the "formula" I had been creating. But it dawned on me, as all good ideas do, that there is really only *one job* during the insight stage. Once this idea came to me, several ideas started "popping up" like a cork held underwater. And that is exactly what the insight stage entails—one job, which is producing lots of ideas and allowing them to surface to the conscious mind.

But that job needs to be further broken down. And so, for this chapter we will purposefully diverge from our usual formula and break down the one job to be done, which is to apply the five types of thinking to produce a large number of creative ideas.

As I stated in chapter 3, the creative process is nonlinear and you will find yourself using various tools in different stages. Keep in mind also that the insight stage may occur during preparation, incubation, and the later stages to come. For the purposes of this book, insight appears here, in the middle. The reality is that we are always generating ideas.

Producing a Large Volume of Ideas

Come up with ideas? Why, that's the easy part! you might be thinking. In some cases, this is true. The world has no shortage of people with ideas—the trouble is making sure those ideas are original, inspired, innovative, and good! Easier said than done. The reality is that producing ideas is a lot more complex than meets the eye. And the reality of great ideas is that they are rare. But to find that rare golden idea, you have to pan a lot of pyrite.

Dean Simonton, a professor of psychology at the University of California, Davis, did extensive research showing that the best way to produce creative ideas is to produce many ideas. Rather than focusing on one single piece of work and "perfecting" it, Simonton recommends creating more, not so much for more's sake but rather because the process of creating itself leads to the "good idea."

I should note that this is different from being productive for productivity's sake. I am not advocating taking on busywork but rather suggesting purposely generating ideas that begin to emerge from the subconscious mind.

Meryl Streep, one of the most decorated actors (winning three Oscars and receiving twenty-one nominations), has appeared in more than seventy films, but that is not all. She also appears on television series, acts and performs onstage, and narrates documentaries and audiobooks. She has starred not only in films that garner award recognition but fan favorites like *Mamma Mia!* and romantic comedies like *It's Complicated*. In fact, the years she was working the most were also the years she won major awards. In 1981, she made *The French Lieutenant's Woman*, *Still of the Night*, *Alice at the Palace*, and *Sophie's Choice*. She ultimately won the Oscar for Best Actress in 1983 for *Sophie's Choice*.

She is hardly alone. Pablo Picasso is said to have painted some twenty thousand pieces. Not all of them are masterpieces and not all of them changed the course of art. Nevertheless, each piece was necessary to his process. Albert Einstein, famous now for his paper on the general theory of relativity, changed our understanding of how we measure space and time. His findings became the foundation of modern physics and quantum mechanics and inspired subsequent research and discoveries—from the atomic bomb and nuclear power to GPS navigation, just to name a few. While that paper was groundbreaking and is now world-renowned, he wrote more than 250 scientific papers during his career. This is an astounding number when you think of all the research required for such papers. Johann Sebastian Bach is said to have composed a cantata *every week*. Even people who don't listen to classical music can recognize his famous Toccata and Fugue in D Minor—made popular by Disney's *Fantasia*. Surely, while not every single one of his compositions was as popular, they were nevertheless integral to his creative process.

In every field, in every art form, in every business office in the world, the best ideas come after many others. Thomas Edison, made famous for his light bulb, had over one thousand patents. Richard Branson, founder of Virgin Atlantic, started some 250 companies. Joyce Carol Oates, who is still writing, has published over fifty-six novels, thirty-nine short story collections, eight poetry collections, five dramas, and nine essay collections. Were all bestsellers? No. Were all Oprah's Book Club picks? No. But she consistently produces the works based on the ideas that come to her.

The question you may have by now, as I do when I think of all these inspiring, prolific, and prodigious individuals, is *how.* How do they keep producing idea after idea? Do they ever tire? Do they ever get stuck or stumped? How do they even do it? That is, how do their brains access and then bring forth these ideas?

While the creative process gives us a method—that is, a cognitive assembly line for producing ideas—the five types of creative thinking, which were first created by Graham Wallas and later refined by other creative geniuses, and which I have synthesized in this book, give us the cognitive tools to move ideas along the assembly line to find the best few ideas or the one best idea.

In order for this large production of ideas to occur, we must split up and study the various types of thinking that produce creative ideas.

Most creative research just lumps "idea production" into one category. But idea production during insight occurs through a combination of two or more of the following types of thinking:

- Divergent
- Convergent
- Lateral
- Aesthetic
- Inspirational

The creative process is nonlinear and you will find yourself using the five types of thinking in different stages. You will produce ideas throughout the preparation, incubation, insight, evaluation, and implementation stages. Producing ideas using these types of thinking, however, is most successful during the insight stage. But don't make the mistake of jumping right into thinking of ideas without having done the work needed for preparation or without taking the conscious "time off" needed for incubation. The reality is that we are *always* generating ideas. No one can control when or from where the ideas emerge. Yes, we can cajole them, but sometimes they will just arise. Don't fight it. Be on alert. Remember there is no straight line. Some researchers of creativity have equated these stages to a zigzag. Even that seems woefully insufficient. Even zigging and zagging implies a "line" with clear bends and connections.

I like to think of these stages in terms of water metaphors, such as waves rising, falling, ebbing, and flowing. Or rivers, branching off in thousands of different directions. Some pour into something bigger. Some end in a muddy swamp. Some encounter clogged pipes, where they wait for a boost or a cleanse of some sort or for someone to simply turn on the faucet. My point is that when ideas are coming, they are flowing. Sometimes, they are dripping. Sometimes, it's like opening a fire hydrant on Second Avenue in the summer. In the remaining chapters, we will discuss how to control the flow of ideas, how to pick the best ones and elaborate on them, how to abandon the ones that have dried up or come to a dead end, and how to find the ones that flow into deeper waters. But for now, we are only concerned with opening the pipes to let them out.

Two of the Types of Thinking Produce a Way to Funnel Ideas

Two types of thinking—divergent and convergent—are used to produce ideas and move them through the insight stage. Divergent thinking (DT) occurs when you let your mind wander to produce as many different ideas as possible that are answers to a question or solutions to a problem. This way of thinking requires you to pull from seemingly unconnected things—different fields of study, different industries, different experiences, and so on. According to J. P. Guilford, the psychologist who coined the terms "convergent thinking" and "divergent thinking" in 1956, divergent thinking involves more creativity. It's easy to feel "all over the place" with this type of thinking.

Convergent thinking (CT) is the opposite of divergent thinking. It occurs when you take your divergent ideas and begin to converge on the right idea as a single answer or solution to a problem. CT focuses on reaching a well-defined idea or solution. This type of thinking is best suited for tasks that involve logic as opposed to creativity, such as answering a multiple-choice question or solving a math problem in which you know there is only one possible solution.

Combined, these types of thinking create a funnel where lots of ideas are generated at the widest part of the funnel (divergent) and flow down to the narrowest part of the funnel (convergent) where the best one or two ideas are reached. As noted above, there are three other types of thinking used to generate ideas, and these can help produce more ideas to throw into the funnel of ideas created through the insight stage. We'll talk more about those types of thinking later in this chapter.

Divergent Thinking

Divergent thinking increases flexibility in how you approach problems. Looking at a problem from many angles or perspectives gets your mind in full gear. It helps you consider all possible options (even if some seem completely unlikely). This is a free-flow form of thinking where no idea is off-limits and the goal is to generate multiple paths forward.

DT is valuable when there is no tried and tested solution readily available or adaptable. When we begin to solve a creative problem in the preparation stage, we use DT.

Not long after the Metropolitan Museum of Art in NYC reopened after COVID, I returned. I have always loved this place. Standing in the Greek and Roman collection, I was all alone and in heaven. I had only experienced these sculptures with the throngs of wall-to-wall visitors that usually cram into the museum. I stopped by the Crouching Aphrodite. We had time alone, something that had seemed impossible in the past. I made some sketches and took some pictures with my phone.

The next morning, I was in my studio and meeting with staff at Atelier Lucca. We began planning an Aphrodite series of our own inspired by my museum visit. We started by making multiple drawings on paper and modeling maquettes (smaller three-dimensional models or rough drafts made in clay or plaster of larger sculptures). Lots of ideas came forth using DT.

During the insight stage, DT comes in handy, because here you are working with a mind full of ideas—ideas that you have gathered during the preparation stage and let germinate and take root in your subconscious during the incubation stage. A simple example of DT occurs when you are shown a photo or a cartoon and asked to think of at least ten captions. You are then forced to create ten different narratives that illustrate the picture. In art or music, DT results in various renderings of a subject or variations in lyrics and melodies.

DT can be enhanced in various ways, such as brainstorming.

Brainstorming

Brainstorming is one of the most effective ways to empty your mind of a certain topic. It's like throwing the proverbial spaghetti up against the wall and seeing what sticks. Speaking of "sticks," one of the best ways to brainstorm, whether alone or with a team, is to use Post-its or a whiteboard. Set a timer (sometimes it helps to have parameters or limitations because this forces people to think rapidly and not hold back) and get out as many ideas as possible. IDEO, a design thinking firm, suggests even putting parameters on the concept itself, forcing people to produce some truly innovative ideas. For example, let's say you have to produce a vehicle—but the parameter or limitation is that you can't use any fuel to operate the vehicle. What alternative energies could it run on?

Mind-mapping is a type of brainstorming for which you take a single idea and write it down in the middle of a whiteboard or large piece of blank paper. From this one idea, you draw branches from a central idea to related ideas.

Convergent Thinking

Unlike divergent thinking, convergent thinking is the process of finding concrete solutions to problems. It is the process of evaluating, selecting, and refining the best ideas produced in DT. CT allows you to sift through ideas, group them into themes, pick out common threads, and decide upon winners and losers—and do so efficiently. Efficiency is especially important when you're under pressure and deadlines are involved; it can prevent decision overload. This type of thinking focuses on coming up with a single, well-established answer to a problem. When an individual is using convergence to solve a problem, they consciously use standards or probabilities to make judgments. This contrasts with DT, in which a person defers judgment while looking for and accepting many possible solutions.

Though seemingly different, DT and CT are opposite sides of the same coin. Whereas DT is about discovering, CT is about defining. You've gathered plenty of information and ideas; now it's time to focus on systematically synthesizing, organizing, and categorizing it all to arrive at a well-defined solution. Now you need a platform or way to apply these kinds of thinking.

You can see how these two types of thinking help you narrow lots of ideas down to a few, but there are three other types of thinking that can help you produce even more ideas to throw into the funnel: lateral, aesthetic, and inspirational thinking.

Lateral Thinking

I think of lateral thinking as similar to divergent thinking with one big difference. Unlike DT, which follows earlier thought patterns, lateral thinking doesn't follow or connect with any earlier thought patterns. For example, if I asked you to produce one hundred uses for a spoon, you might be thinking, *A spoon is a spoon; it delivers food to the mouth.* But lateral thinking requires you to go outside the norms of a spoon's use. Suddenly a spoon could be a paintbrush, a tool for gardening, a doorstop, a bookmark, and so on. Soon you may even find you've invented an entirely new use that you've never thought of before.

Lateral thinking is often the result of a happy accident. You may not have thought of a certain use until you see it. Remember the Velcro story from the preparation chapter? George de Mestral didn't expect to invent Velcro when he went on a walk with his dog in the Swiss Alps. The key factor was his ability to be curious about the burs stuck all over his dog. By looking at them closely under a microscope, he was able to observe and replicate the small hooks that get snagged in clothing. Sometimes, to use lateral thinking, you have to be on alert for opportunities to do so.

In 1984, two former street performers, Guy Laliberté and Gilles Ste-Croix, from a small city in Quebec, Canada, didn't set out to transform the circus business model. They simply wondered, *What if we created a circus experience that looked like no other circus?* Prior to their new idea, most people waited for an annual visit from a traveling circus. Tents went up and, usually by railcar or caravan, circus animals and performers rolled into town. Most of us have at least one memory of a circus coming to town or have watched movies such as *The Greatest Showman*, about P. T. Barnum, the creator of the Ringling Bros. and Barnum & Bailey Circus. Within the tent, there are any number of acrobatics, animal tricks, and acts going on, and of course there are clowns. It's typically a sensory overload. Each event occurring in the ring is disconnected from the others. But these Canadians wanted to do it differently. They wanted to remove the animals—considering their tricks a problematic and inhumane practice—along with the idea of "freaks," and have what they called a "proper circus." The emphasis would be on acrobatics—death-defying trapeze artistry would be combined with elegant dance, music, and costumes to tell a story. They wondered, *What if venue, costumes, sets, music, lights, clowns, and audience could work together to tell a narrative?* The result was Cirque du Soleil, translated as "circus of the sun." It quite literally grew to be the largest circus under the sun. It has had multiple permanent Las Vegas shows, playing to more than 9,500 people a night. Since its inception, nearly 100 million visitors have seen fifty-plus varieties of shows. Instead of the circus coming to town, people now travel from all over the world to see the circus—and that circus brings in 5 percent of Las Vegas's annual revenue. Cirque du Soleil is not a circus that we know from our childhoods. It is a whole new idea of what a circus can be.

Aesthetic Thinking

Aesthetic thinking is about the appreciation of art and beauty. This type of creative thinking produces ideas that are beautiful and pleasant to our senses. The potential for this type of creative thinking is and has always been embedded within all humans. I can't help but think of our ancestors, who some twenty thousand years ago felt so inspired to express themselves and their stories that they created cave art. For as long as we have been human, we have used aesthetic, creative thinking in all kinds of ways, including but not limited to:

- **Visual and Spatial Compositions:** Painters, sculptors, architects, photographers, graphic designers, and mixed-media artists use creative ideas to produce structures, compositions, colors, and forms.
- **Music:** Composers, musicians, vocalists, and even digital artists and DJs use creative ideas to produce tempos, rhythms, and melodies for musical output.
- **Storytelling:** Novelists, nonfiction writers, memoirists, biographers, poets, screenwriters, and content creators (bloggers, journalists, advertisers, and so on) use creative ideas to produce dramas, comedies, and dialogue to express the human condition with the written word.
- **Scientific Advancements:** Mathematicians, physicists, and chemists use creative ideas to produce elegant equations, impressive inventions, discoveries, and life-changing pharmaceuticals, among many other things.

Work that is built on aesthetic creative thinking can produce a painting and build a story, but it can also design a house or generate a unique branding and marketing campaign. Whether your idea is for a great work of art, a new song, or a new logo, aesthetic thinking needs to be combined with the other types of creative thinking. Even the developers in our Cirque du Soleil example harnessed aesthetic thinking in addition to other types of thinking. Remember that ideas are based on combinations, which in turn help you see relationships.

Inspirational Thinking

Inspirational thinking involves getting creative ideas from someone or somewhere else. This type of creative thinking can happen in dreams or sudden bursts of clarity: a special experience when everything comes together and makes sense in one moment (the "aha moment"). While most ideas are not a result of "epiphanies," as we've discussed, there are times when an "inspired" idea does reveal itself. Many artists swear by such moments. Giacomo Puccini famously announced, "The music of this opera [*Madame Butterfly*] was dictated to me by God. I was merely instrumental in getting it on paper and communicating it to the public." And Neil Simon swore, "I don't write consciously—it is as if the muse sits on my shoulder." Even Paul McCartney, who wrote "Yesterday" in 1964, claims the song came to him in a dream. He recalls:

> I was living in a little flat at the top of a house, and I had a piano by my bed. I woke up one morning with a tune in my head and I thought "Hey, I don't know this tune—or do I?" It was like a jazz melody. My dad used to know a lot of old jazz tunes; I thought maybe I just remembered it from the past. I went to the piano and found the chords to it, made sure I

> remembered it, and then hawked it 'round to all my friends, asking what it was: "Do you know this? It's a good little tune, but I couldn't have written it because I dreamt it."[1]

The sculptor Alberto Giacometti, who had been working in cubism and surrealism, had become despondent with his own artwork. He felt he was just turning out the same art over and over. Then one winter night in Paris in 1945, he went to a newsreel theater on Boulevard du Montparnasse. As he sat in the dingy theater, he watched a video of a destroyed Europe starting to rebuild itself, but then something happened to him. "Suddenly I no longer knew just what it was I could see on the screen," he said. "Instead of figures moving in a three-dimensional space I saw only black and white specks shifting on a flat surface. They had lost all meaning. I looked at the people around me and suddenly I saw them as I've never seen them before."

Giacometti suddenly saw the world a different way. He hurried out of the theater and onto the street. Everything that had previously been so familiar now looked different. He recalled, "The boulevard had the beauty of the *Arabian Nights.* Everything was different, space and objects and colors and the silence, because this sense of space generates silence, and bathes objects in silence. That day completely revaluated reality for me. It became the unknown, a marvelous unknown."[2]

The experience produced a fundamental change in Giacometti's work. He left cubism and surrealism and developed now-iconic art that

---

1. Beatles Bible, "Yesterday." *The Beatles Bible.* Accessed January 5, 2026. https://www.beatlesbible.com/songs/yesterday/.

2. Charlie Connelly, "Alberto Giacometti and the moment that transformed his art," *The New European* (The New World website), January 10, 2021, https://www.thenewworld.co.uk/brexit-news-the-great-life-of-alberto-giacometti-6875184.

was uniquely his—elongated figures of men and women with rough surfaces that cover the long arms and legs.

Sometimes these extraordinary experiences are called "channeling." This term implies that someone else, a higher spirit, is involved in producing the creative revelation or idea. Steven Pressfield, in his books on creativity, recommends that if it troubles you to think of "angels" or a "higher power," try thinking of these as "angels in abstract"—meaning you don't have to "name them," but rather you can just be open to any kind of ineffable mystical experience. In other words: Don't question it. If it comes to you, thank whatever it was that was responsible for it, and move on. Don't disregard it because you can't name or know the source. Allow space for the unexpected, and the unexpected is bound to happen.

The Insight Archetype: Thinker

Our behavior manifests in the way we appear to the outside world, in what we say and what we do. The Thinker's behavior produces and connects creative ideas—lots of them. I think this quote from Peter Senge, systems scientist at MIT, describes the Thinker's behavior at its best: "a discipline for seeing wholes rather than the parts, for seeing patterns of change, rather than static snapshots, and for understanding the subtle interconnectedness that gives systems their unique character."[3]

The Thinker's behavior starts with understanding the relationship between the parts and how they work together (synthesizing) and then proceeds to focus on the individual parts (analyzing). This behavior is constant whether the challenge concerns a bicycle, a company, or

---

3. Peter M. Senge, *The Fifth Discipline: The Art and Practice of the Learning Organization* (Doubleday, 1990), 68.

the making of a sculpture. The Thinker displays several characteristics: curiosity, open-mindedness, courage, and perspicacity.

Curiosity

The Thinker is curious. Curiosity is perhaps the greatest driver of creativity. It pushes us to understand things right in front of us as well as worlds we can't quite see. As humans, it has allowed us to adapt and survive. In individual beings, curiosity produces a similar force. Curious people are those who can produce lots of ideas, which, in turn, allows them to better handle uncertainty, vagueness, and unconventionality. Curious people do not use criticism as a starting point. Instead, they ask themselves, *What am I not seeing? What am I missing? What's under the iceberg that I'm not seeing?* They ask questions and don't assume they know the answer, which leads to the next behavior.

Open-Mindedness

Thinkers are good listeners. They don't try to formulate the answer when someone is talking or try to jump in and one-up the speaker. They don't try to share their own experience right away; rather, they want to learn more about why a person thinks the way they do. They don't get defensive or argumentative when listening to others' ideas, nor are they quick to shut down others' experiences. They keep an open mind and try to get to the root of the issue. They don't try to assert dominance or claim to know everything. They stay humble. They seek not to be right but to understand. And if they can't understand, at the very least they recognize why or how someone came to their conclusions. In other words, they practice keeping their mouth shut and stay as present as possible.

Courage

It takes great courage to think deeply through problems. Sometimes it means asking tough questions that no one else wants to ask. It takes courage to ask someone personal questions. Not every doctor wants to address the elephant in their exam room. Sometimes it's clear that a patient is depressed, drinking, or eating too much. It's often easier to simply operate on the leg and not deal with the whole person.

When it comes to art, creation, and business, it takes courage to look deeper. Writers and composers know this intimately. It takes courage to write down one's thoughts—the fear of reprisal, rejection, or judgment is real. No one wants to be criticized or be called out as a fool, or worse, a hack. To create something new, to produce new ideas, takes real courage. It may even mean being laughed at. In the 1750s, after a trip to France, Jonas Hanway brought back to England something he called an "umbrella"—a small, waterproof, lightweight version of the parasol used mostly by French women to block the sun. He was using it to keep dry. As a man carrying one, he was laughed at and ridiculed, and reports claim people threw things at him. It took almost fifty years for jolly old and very wet English people to stop laughing and pop open umbrellas to keep dry too.

Failure-to-adapt business stories are also legendary. Blockbuster and its die-hard fans were sure Netflix and digital streaming would be a fad. Kodak kept cranking out film as the digital revolution was in full swing. Borders kept building brick-and-mortar bookstores as Jeff Bezos moved Amazon out of his garage and into a warehouse. The history books are filled with intrepid and bold spirits who took the first step while many were laughing and, in many cases, altogether ignorant of the innovators' moves. Don't let others' opinions stop you. Don't let fear of failure stop you. A Thinker still has worries and fears, a natural consequence of thinking through all the possible outcomes, but they don't let that stop them. They have courage and keep pressing on.

Perspicacity

The Thinker is perspicacious—in other words, a big-picture Thinker. They don't paint on the proverbial small notepad; rather, they could fill an entire wall with their visions and thoughts. They are willing to expand the range of options available for solving a problem. They see things from the ten-thousand- or thirty-thousand-foot range. They look ahead five, ten, fifteen, one hundred years. They aren't sidetracked by small details. They think beyond today, themselves, and the boundaries currently known. They are willing to push themselves outside their current understanding—or even capabilities.

In the 1890s, Nikola Tesla began pursuing his ideas for wireless lighting and global wireless electric power. He started conducting high-voltage, high-frequency power experiments. By 1893, he proclaimed the possibility of wireless communication. He envisioned his Wardenclyffe Tower, an intercontinental wireless communication and power transmitter, but he lacked the funding and backing to see it through to completion. He died in New York City in 1943, leaving behind a pile of unpaid bills and debts, and fell into obscurity. As we all know now, wireless communication was indeed possible. He was perspicacious enough to see that, even if he didn't make it possible in his lifetime. Sometimes the best ideas are built on the shoulders of giants whom the world once laughed at.

The "One for All and All for One" Creativity Myth

We truly don't work alone—we need a team, as well as our time alone. Most great ideas can't be executed on one's own. Tesla knew this. He needed a team, money, and backing. Without these, his ideas remained on the page.

Solitary and Mingling Time: Rubens and Bass

Peter Paul Rubens, a Flemish painter, lived four hundred years ago. He lived and worked in Antwerp after spending important years honing his craft in Italy. Meanwhile, his brother became a politician and married into a family of importance. Rubens was then able to use his connections to get himself named court painter for the rulers of the Netherlands.

Was Rubens a great painter? Without a doubt. He was also a great painter who was able to attract other great painters to work with him and around him. He also spent a good deal of time on the road as a diplomat for his government and, while doing so, sold art to a lot of very wealthy patrons.

In modern times, Ron Bass is an Academy Award–winning screenwriter. His sixteen films have brought in over $2 billion. But he doesn't do all his writing by himself. He has a team of six writers along with researchers who help him draft storyboards, write scripts, and perform other duties. He pulls it all together and is the marquee name.

Bass started writing at six years old but stopped after a teacher criticized his work. He did not resume writing until he was thirty-two years old. He spent seventeen years as an entertainment lawyer, until he started screenwriting at forty-two. He's now in such demand that he can employ that large staff. But he also works independently of them and writes up to fourteen hours per day himself. So, in many ways, people like Edison, Michelangelo, Rubens, and Bass weren't only creators. They were great entrepreneurs and team builders. They used their names to develop a brand that was actually the result of collaborative operations.

Summary: Are People More Creative When They Work Alone or Together?

As Hans Rookmaaker said in *Art Needs No Justification*, "Everyone knows that a good performance is never the work of one person alone, but that he needed the help of many others."[4] Beyoncé would agree with Hans. Her album *Lemonade*, released in 2016, credits seventy-two writers and was recorded between June 2014 and July 2015 across eleven studios in the United States.

The debate between producing ideas alone and collaborating has been ongoing. It can be tracked down to two significant books: *Quiet* and *Group Genius*. In 2016, Susan Cain wrote *Quiet: The Power of Introverts in a World That Can't Stop Talking*. She argues that we dramatically undervalue introverts and shows how much we lose in doing so. While collaborating is the new "in thing" for creative idea production, Cain argues that history has demonstrated the importance of solitude as well as collaboration for achieving breakthrough ideas.

Keith Sawyer, author of *Group Genius: The Creative Power of Collaboration* (first published in 2007 and revised in 2017) takes the middle-of-the-road approach. His research shows that while teams are better than individuals at solving complex problems, most creative people are both introverted and extroverted.

In my humble opinion, but based on extensive experience, this is how it works for me: I am best at creative thinking when I spend solitary time first and then spend time with my team. I need to move between being alone and spending time with my team, and back again.

You will find the need to call on others' opinions and ideas especially important as you move into the next stage—evaluation.

---

4. Hans R. Rookmaaker, *Art Needs No Justification* (InterVarsity Press, 1978), 32.

CASE STUDY

Insight in Action: Driving a UPS Truck and Discovering New Models for Healthcare Logistics

It may be surprising to learn that individuals involved in healthcare delivery spend a considerable amount of time on creative work, be it on the clinical or administrative side. Designing a patient form requires creativity, as does determining the best layout for a hospital or a medical office building. When administrators design a new, more simplified and efficient check-in process, that, too, takes creativity. These are just a few examples of how tapping into your creativity can be beneficial even in fields or professions that are not typically thought of as creative. Embracing creativity in the workplace involves cultivating different ways of thinking and different approaches to problem-solving. In this case study, I will explain how we used different types of creative thinking to study healthcare and to ultimately build an innovative healthcare delivery network.

On a cold January afternoon, the clinic was busy. I was only one hour into seeing patients and already behind schedule. I walked into the exam room and apologized to the patient, Jim, for my tardiness. Jim explained that he had been having right-knee pain for a week. But of late, it had gotten so bad that he worried about missing work. He was a truck driver. His wife then explained that he had been limping around like an old man for at least a month and complaining to her the entire time. She had talked to a friend who was a nurse and had been given my name. She had made the appointment.

I examined his knee. It was swollen and stiff. He winced when I palpated the inner side. X-rays showed some early arthritis. My diagnosis was a torn meniscus, but I needed an MRI to confirm this. I asked him why he had waited so long to see someone. He explained that his employer provided health insurance, but the deductible was so high he feared he would have to go into his savings to cover the costs of treating his injury. This was a story I would hear time and time again from patients. Healthcare, in spite of some reforms, including access to insurance through the Affordable Care Act, is still out of reach for many.

When I graduated from engineering school in 1969, approximately 7 percent of America's GDP was being spent on healthcare. In 2007, when HCDS broke ground for its second specialty hospital, 17 percent of America's GDP was being spent on healthcare. In 2020, America spent almost 19.7 percent of its GDP on healthcare—that adds up to about $4.1 trillion, or $12,530 per individual.

With this rising expense, three conditions remain present:

1. Medicare costs continue to grow and to this day are secondary only to defense spending in the United States.
2. If city and town governments take into account the contractual commitments, including healthcare, for retired employees, many are actually near bankruptcy.
3. The cost of providing healthcare for employees, their families, and retirees often threatens the competitiveness of American companies on a global scale.

Using Divergent Thinking and Convergent Thinking to Produce Ideas

My business studies included the work of Clay Christensen at Harvard Business School on what he called "disruptive innovation." Christensen, whom I met and whose lectures I attended, became a mentor of mine. He taught me that the challenge I was facing was not new. Other companies have needed to transform expensive, complicated products and services into those that are lower in cost, more accessible, and higher in quality. Christensen encouraged me to study companies outside healthcare to produce ideas I needed for healthcare solutions. That is exactly what I did.

The intersection here was not just of disciplines but of different successful business cultures within HCDS. Some of the "businesses" at work within HCDS included revenue cycle management, clinical providers (doctors, therapists, nurses, physician's assistants), process improvement, the solution center, IT, marketing and communications, and asset management. All the teams shared a common goal of delivering the best patient experience. This "intersection" of cultures resulted in breakthrough divergent ideas and innovation in the delivery of services to our patients.

Driving Around Town in a Brown Truck

One source of divergent ideas for me came from studying successful, established companies—both on paper and on-site. It was the on-site visits and the chats with employees and managers in which they explained their processes that gave me the ideas I could eventually converge into solutions.

A company I admired at the time, and still do, is UPS. I remember having long chats with regional managers as they described the logistics that drove their regional service centers. At some point, I reached out to them and asked if they would mind if I observed their process in action. My eyes were really opened the hot summer day I put on a UPS uniform, jumped into a brown truck, and helped deliver packages. Except for working in the back of the truck, which was as hot as an oven, I enjoyed the long day in which I observed well-planned and flawlessly executed routes and deliveries. Everyone I encountered had a "better, not bigger" philosophy, and everyone emphasized customer-first solutions. Their guiding question was, What was best for the customer? I was impressed. I then encouraged HCDS clinicians from different subfields (physicians, physical therapists, athletic trainers, and others) to make these worksite visits and record their observations.

Doing Our Mind-Mapping

Following our on-site visits to UPS, my HCDS associates and I engaged in a session of mind-mapping to generate ideas for building our upstart based on what we had observed. Each of us scribbled our UPS observations onto Post-it Notes, and we placed these notes into labeled cardboard boxes. We then drew Post-its from the boxes and placed them on a number of whiteboards around a conference room. These ideas were "intersected" with those of other HCDS associates to come up with a convergence of solutions.

In the late eighties and early nineties, the journey I took on the brown truck started our organization thinking about how UPS drivers should be thought of as athletes. In fact, we started thinking of employees as "industrial athletes," a term that swept through occupational health circles. This concept was a way of thinking in orthopedics and occupational medicine about work-related injuries or injured individuals across various industries who must return to a highly physical job. The approach was to treat these patients similarly to the way you would treat an injured athlete who has to return to a specific sport and level of function (above and beyond everyday activities). This means that athletes and highly physical workers with similar diagnoses would get the same level of care and surgery. And the focus would be on the rehab and training needed to recover and return to their higher level of function (job or sport).

This was a successful intersection of cultures—UPS (package delivery) + HCDS (healthcare delivery).

Summary: A Connected Family of Cross-Field (XF) Teams

At HCDS, different departments within each of the clinical administrative divisions work together to reach a shared goal, such as building a new hospital in a distant community. These XF teams of physicians, nurses, architects, lawyers, accountants, and others worked to remain on schedule and ensure quality.

By using a systems and design approach to idea production, people had a wider perspective on their particular roles at HCDS. Fragmentation—that is, focusing only on specific departments—was avoided and *the patient experience was kept central.*

XF teams at HCDS were an important part of producing ideas for both uncovering problems and developing solutions for those problems. These teams were composed of people from different disciplines, especially those with clinical and administrative professionals.

When you were part of these HCDS teams, systems thinking made you look closely at how you interacted with individual members of the team as well as how you worked with the team as a whole.

Jump-Start Your Creativity

Writing prompts for your journal:

- Spend some time brainstorming or mind-mapping an idea or ideas you have prepared for and have been incubating.
- How can you use lateral thinking, aesthetic thinking, or systems thinking to generate more ideas?
- Would you say you get your best ideas on your own or with others? Take an honest assessment of yourself. Do you work better with others or alone? Why?

- If you have determined you work better with others and currently find yourself working alone, what can you do to make sure you have more time with others? Or if you find you do better on your own, but are constantly with others, how can you find a balance and carve out some time for yourself to generate ideas?
- How are you keeping the user/patient/customer/client/audience central in your approach to producing solutions?
- How can you apply a systems approach to your solution? Are you focused too closely on one specific area or fragment of your work? Have you thought of all the possible touchpoints?
- Who are you working with, or who can you ask to work with or observe, to make sure you're getting a complete picture of the problem and solution?

CHAPTER 7

Stage 4: Evaluation

Steve Jobs worked for and was fired by Apple before returning to lead the company through a massive transformation. Few people can forget his 2007 announcement of the world's first iPhone—where on the stage he gleefully pronounced: "An iPod, a phone, and internet mobile communicator . . . these are *not* three separate devices! And we are calling it iPhone! Today Apple is going to reinvent the phone. And here it is." Standing onstage in his signature jeans and black turtleneck, Jobs held up his iPhone. While this might be hard to believe for the young people out there, the world was incredulous. Up until that moment, we had Blackberries—devices from which you could email and call people or slowly search the internet. We also had iPods, another device to carry around, for listening to music. And don't forget, we also had cameras and video cameras. And now, suddenly,

Jobs stood before the world and basically said, "Here, take the entire world and carry it in your pocket."

He used his vast experience and pulled together a team of engineers from various fields—mobile phone, internet, music, and don't forget design—to produce the iPhone. Steve Jobs was twenty-one years old in 1976 when he started Apple with Steve Wozniak. But it was only after he was fired from Apple and worked in different industries that he was able to return and in 2007 create the iPhone.

The great masters of creativity have not only innovative ideas but also experience—they are not the newest and most popular or sought-after "artist of the moment." I often laugh when I read a review about a "new and upcoming" artist fresh out of school. I know, from my own experience, that what is being prized or revered is not so much the artist's work itself but the "it" factor of the artist, or rather the efficacy of their PR team or their school's or gallery's PR team. In contrast, I think of Pierre-Auguste Renoir, who was almost fifty years old before he was recognized and began to make a name for himself. The Salon de Paris rejected Renoir. He and his peers Claude Monet, Édouard Manet, Edgar Degas, Paul Cézanne, and Camille Pissarro went on to form the Anonymous Society of Painters, Sculptors, and Engravers, or what we now call the impressionists. Renoir was thirty-six years old at the time—and still getting rejected. That didn't stop him, though. He continued to paint alongside his friend Monet and work on his technique. On a trip to Italy in 1881, while admiring and studying the Renaissance masters, including Raphael, Renoir decided to combine the impressionistic style that he had perfected over years of experience with that of classicism—and what came out of it was his popular and well-received Ingresque period. His paintings depicted classical figures in the foreground against the background of his impressionistic landscapes. Time, patience, experience, creativity, and the combination of ideas led to this new era for him.

During Stages 1 through 3 of the creative process, we prepared ourselves for, observed, and cultivated ideas. We also went through a number of Jobs to Be Done with the aim of generating new ideas, incubating them, and then analyzing them. In Stage 4, evaluation, we will start to put everything together, to "connect the dots," if you will. In Stage 4, to produce truly creative, disruptive, transformative ideas, you have two remaining Jobs to Be Done: connecting or combining ideas and then choosing the best combination of these ideas, which I call "converging."

Many times, when the creative process is discussed, the insight stage, when ideas are generated, gets all the credit. But Stage 4, evaluation, discussed in this chapter, and stage 5, implementation, discussed in the next chapter, are also crucially important for creativity.

When we discussed the insight stage, we saw numerous ideas and combinations of ideas materialize in our consciousness. Many of these ideas would not turn out to be adequate solutions for our creative problem. A new business model may not be financially appropriate, a sculptural idea may turn out to be ordinary, and an idea for a group of operating rooms might be inefficient.

To be successful creators, we must be able to *choose* which ideas to discard and which ones to keep. The JTBD in Stage 4 will help you do so.

JTBD 1: Connect and Combine Ideas

Creativity that truly makes a difference almost never comes from a single idea. The best creative solutions emerge from combined or connected ideas, and often these connections are hidden and are not apparent at first sight. Charles Darwin had no idea that when he stumbled upon birds in the Galápagos, he would uncover the foundations of human life, let alone entirely new fields of study. In this first JTBD, you begin to connect or combine ideas from your own knowledge, experience, and creativity. Innovators like Twyla Tharp and Steve Jobs believed that creativity was the bringing together of two or more ideas. In a 1996 interview with *Wired*, Jobs said, "Creativity is just connecting things. When you ask people how they did something, they feel a little guilty because they didn't really do it, they just saw something."[1] But he added that the reason those connections could even be made was *experience.* Acquiring knowledge and a variety of experiences allows you to have a source of ideas. Experience is important for readily making connections. When you have had more experiences than others or have thought more about your experiences, you can more easily connect ideas, experiences, and flashes of insight and be more creative.

Below is the process used by Renoir, Jobs, Darwin, and all the great creators who have gone before them. They essentially collected ideas they gathered from experience, knowledge, study, and applications. They then went on to connect the ideas. Then, after isolating the right set of ideas, they essentially chose which ideas to elaborate upon.

Knowledge: Collecting Ideas

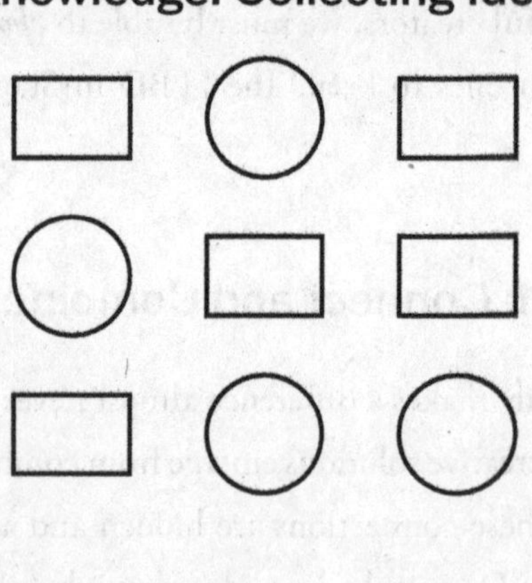

1. Steve Jobs, interview by Gary Wolf, "Steve Jobs: The Next Insanely Great Thing," *Wired*, February 1996, https://www.wired.com/1996/02/jobs-2/.

Experience: Connecting Ideas

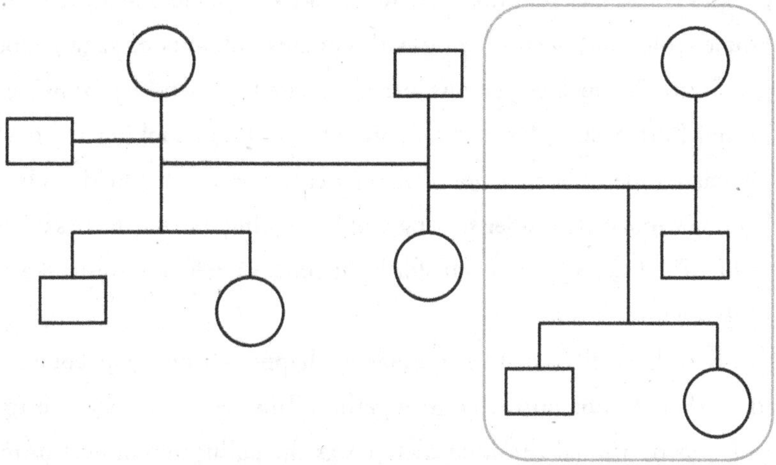

Creativity: Isolating the Right Set of Connecting Ideas

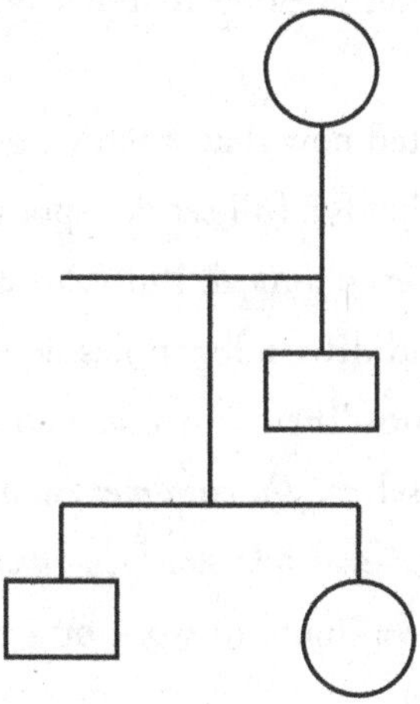

Related Ideas Versus Unrelated Ideas

Within the realm of combining ideas, there are those that normally go together and those that don't normally go together.

Oreo cookies are an example of related ideas; most people enjoy cookies with a glass of milk—or cream. What happens when you combine cookies and cream (along with copious amounts of sugar)? You get Oreos. People love peanuts and chocolate together—hence Reese's Peanut Butter Cups. It's easy to look to the world of cooking and food for related ideas, but it's not always so easy outside this field. Rollerblading came out of roller skating and ice skating. How can ice skaters train off the ice? Why not transform the roller skate to an in-line skate? Makes sense.

But the really creative gymnastics happens when you combine ideas that do not normally go together. This requires what is often called associational thinking, defined as the ability to connect unrelated things. This combining of unrelated ideas (think: how Darwin combined the study of birds with geology or Jobs combined the mobile phone with a computer) is foundational to creativity. Combining things that normally don't belong together allows us to change the paradigm completely.

We take it for granted now that when we go on road trips, we can count on a gas station that is a full-service spot to get not just gas but a coffee, some snacks, or even a meal. But years ago, you would need to fill up your gas tank and drive a few miles down the road to get your coffee at Dunkin' Donuts. Then someone who put their design thinking cap on said to themselves, *The customer has a need for both coffee and gas at roughly the same time, so why not bring them together?* No one can imagine starting their commute to work or a road trip without a gas station with full amenities.

In 1995, a young man by the name of Larry Page was considering Stanford for grad school, and Sergey Brin, a student there, showed him around the campus. Years later, the two admitted to disagreeing about nearly everything at their first meeting. But Page eventually enrolled at Stanford and the two came together for a united goal. Working out of their dorm rooms, the two were busy combining two disparate ideas: ranking systems and citations in academic journals. But they wanted to use these two disparate ideas to clear up the clutter of the early World Wide Web and make the web more searchable. Was there some way to sort through and determine the importance of all the burgeoning websites? They, in their own words, wanted "to organize the world's information and make it universally accessible and useful."

To do so, the two men had to build their own server. Talk about combining ideas: they didn't have much money or time, but they did have Legos—so, you guessed it, they built their server tower out of Legos. In fact, you can go to Stanford and see the server built out of Legos for yourself. It's argued to be the world's "most expensive" Lego project in history. It is essentially the size of an average desktop computer tower. The reason it is so precious and expensive is that the company that server helped launch was renamed Google. Today, Google is so synonymous with the word "search" that it is often used as a verb. Go and google that . . . I'll wait. Google is much more than a search engine today—the company owns YouTube, Android, and Gmail. We'd be hard-pressed to think of life without Google. Most of us can't get through a conversation without stopping to check something out on Google. And yet, Google sprouted from the minds of two individuals who came together to solve a problem—by combining two different ideas to create one revolutionary and transformative concept.

JTBD 2: Choose the Best Combination of Ideas

We call this stage "evaluation" for good reason. To evaluate means to form an idea of the amount, number, or value, or simply *to assess.* In order to be productive in executing this job, you must thoroughly understand and assess the combined ideas you have collected through the previous stages and then ask yourself some questions:

- *Is this idea combination really critical?*
- *Has it been used before?*
- *Will it help me solve my problem?*

When choosing the best idea combinations, there needs to be an equilibrium between the spawning of idea combinations (divergent thinking) and the critical evaluation of these ideas (convergent thinking).

Eventually, you will reach a point where a continued push for ideas results in a loss of efficiency and efficacy. This is a time to stop and focus on some trimming. In other words, it's time to turn to "converge." This convergence of ideas has been explained in previous chapters. Here we compare, rank, clump, and occasionally disregard in order to produce a few terrific idea combinations. We essentially become our own personal Google, ranking our ideas to get to the top one or two we can work with.

But be careful not to throw the baby out with the bathwater! You might have a need for your unused ideas. I keep a notebook just for those.

Balancing Quantity with Quality

When we brainstorm in order to generate lots of ideas and their combinations, the aim is to have no limitation on idea generation—the crazier the idea, the better. Or is it?

Remember the Amphicar (the car-boat), the cigarette pack holder smoker (a large pipelike contraption that allowed a person to smoke an entire pack of cigarettes at once), Goodyear's glowing tires (illuminated rubber tires), or the Pluto Lamp (part gas lamp, part vending machine, which dispensed hot water, coffee, tea, or beef stock)? Chances are you don't remember these products because they never took off. Crazy didn't add up to better. Sometimes crazy is just crazy.

Smoking twenty-four cigarettes at once or getting your beef stock from the lamppost outside your house sounds crazy because it is.

That is why, when brainstorming, you might want to tame down the crazy. In brainstorming sessions that I have led, I have found that the crazier the ideas, the less meaningful the combinations arrived at are. Stating idea parameters right from the beginning allows you to arrive at creativity in a more efficient manner. Once again, it's all about choosing. Here, you're choosing to stay away from foolish ideas and to focus on ideas that may provide solutions. This means setting up some guardrails that will help you distinguish foolish ideas from viable ones.

In order to set up these guardrails and weed out unviable ideas, ask the following questions of your creative ideas:

- *How will this help solve a defined problem?*
- *Is this useful/usable?*
- *Can this be executed, elaborated upon, and replicated?*
- *Can this be made affordable and widely available?*
- *Does this appeal only to a small segment of the desired audience?*
- *Is this different just for the sake of being different?*

Remember that we must produce lots of ideas and that only a small percentage will be helpful in solving the problem. Therefore, continuous editing—that is, choosing—is critical to the creative process. What might appear to be a poor idea at first sight might prove helpful when we later combine other ideas with it and look back at it with fresh eyes.

Think Differently About Failure

In order to become adept at choosing between good and bad idea combinations, successful creators must keep an open mind and not get too obsessed with any particular idea. Every creative person must get comfortable with walking away. This, of course, takes courage in a world where walking away, or giving up on an idea, is equated to failing.

When you make choosing a part of the creative process, you soon realize that small failures along the way help steer you in new directions. The less attached you are to a single idea, the easier it is to turn any loss into a gain. Take chocolate chip cookies, for example. They are a result of a baking catastrophe. Ruth Graves Wakefield, the Toll House Inn co-owner, was in the midst of preparing a batch of chocolate cookies for her guests. She ran out of baker's chocolate and thought to chop up a block of Nestlé semisweet chocolate. She had hoped it would melt and spread in the batter while baking. Instead, when she pulled out the cookies, the chips remained intact. Instead of throwing out the entire batch and calling it a day, she served the first-ever batch of homemade chocolate chip cookies to her guests. To her and her guests' delight, the cookies were a sensation.

I had a similar experience while working on the last piece in my Venus sculpture series. These pieces tended more toward the figurative, even though I am generally happiest when my work contains both figurative and abstract elements. The clay had dried and we were about to move the Venus into the kiln for firing. Suddenly the stand on which the heavy sculpture stood collapsed. The artwork fell to the ground and broke into a number of pieces. My fellow artists working with me in the studio stood stunned and our faces froze in horror. Many hours of work had just gone down the drain. Or had they?

I asked that the pieces not be moved. I grabbed my iPhone and started taking pictures of the pile of different-sized fragments. Here was some of the abstraction I had been looking for! The result was a new series of Venus that reflected the equilibrium between figurative and abstract that we had been seeking. We saved some of the pieces and created a new sculpture with the fragments. Out of the fragments of one, I created a group of new pieces. Similarly, in business, it's about breaking apart processes and building newer, preferably better, ones by doing so.

Creativity is part thinking on your feet and part allowing for things to go wrong and adjusting accordingly. The best cooks and bakers know how to quickly substitute when something goes missing from the cupboard. Science, too, has had many unexpected "failures" turn out to be life-changing inventions. Wilson Greatbatch, an adjunct professor of engineering at the State University of New York at Buffalo, was working on building a piece of equipment that was intended to record heart sounds. He failed to do so because he used the wrong transistor. But what he discovered was that instead of recording sounds, his device gave off electrical impulses, mimicking the pacing of the heart. Since he was an engineer, he knew he needed to combine his discovery with the knowledge and experience of a heart surgeon, so he teamed up with William Chardack, a surgeon at Buffalo's Veterans Administration hospital. In 1960, they presented the world with the first pacemaker, which revolutionized the field of cardiology. Thanks to this device, millions of people suffering from serious arrhythmias, fainting, atrial fibrillation, and in some cases cardiac arrest can live healthy and long lives.

Creative Failure

Sometimes, your efforts don't have the expected outcome, and what you get is not the pleasing alternative of a batch of chocolate chip cookies. Sometimes, you just hit a dead end. It can feel, in the moment, quite devastating—even overwhelming. History is filled with stories of great artists who were mentally crushed by their perception of the experience of failure. Because, indeed, it wasn't the failure that weighed on them—it was their perception of it. Will Gompertz, in *Think Like an Artist*, writes:

> This is about the real thing that has happened to us all and we wish it hadn't; the embarrassing, debilitating, and deeply unpleasant experience of feeling a failure. It is about the days, weeks, and years after your project has crashed ingloriously at your feet, leaving you with a crumpled heap of ideas and experiences to sift through for any fragments that might be worth salvaging. It's about the notion of failure in the context of creativity."[2]

The type of failure he describes is different from making a mistake. We can learn from that mistake. But this perception of failure as the end can feel catastrophic, especially if our identity has somehow become linked to the pursuit of this idea. Many people who have lost jobs or companies know this feeling of failure. Perhaps they saw themselves as an "entrepreneur"—they called themselves one, they had the business cards, their name was on the building—and then suddenly, it's all gone. The business. The years of hard work. The contacts. The prestige. It all feels like it added up to nothing. And then come the shame, embarrassment, and feelings of worthlessness. These are followed by the catastrophic and paralyzing belief that because they failed at this one thing, they must be a failure at everything they set out to do. This, of course, is a delusion and a lie, but it's nevertheless how failure feels. It feels permanent—like it will last forever. It feels pervasive—it affects every area of your life. And it feels personal—like only you alone have been targeted by some outside cosmic force to fail. Together, these feelings are paralyzing. These "four P's" (paralyzing, permanent, pervasive, and personal) are what I like to think of as the Depression Starter Kit. Once you fall down this rabbit hole of self-defeating self-talk, it's

2. Will Gompertz, *Think Like an Artist: And Lead a More Creative, Productive Life* (Penguin Books, 2015), 45.

very hard to climb out, and it's best to nip it in the bud. And the best way to do that is to depersonalize the failure.

We Are Not Failures

Let's flip the script on failure. All creatives have had the experience of being rejected or failing to measure up to a preconceived idea or vision of what they had hoped would happen. Long before he became a "Shark" investor, Mark Cuban experienced several failures. His first venture as a bar owner ended in failure. It was closed down. He tried his hand at working at a software store and was fired. Nevertheless, he learned valuable lessons from each experience. His determination led him to start MicroSolutions, a software reselling company, which he later sold for a substantial profit, paving the way for where he is today, a billionaire investor.

This is why it's so important to depersonalize the failure of a creative endeavor. When failure occurs during the creative process, we *feel* like we failed, but we are not sure what we personally did to cause the failure or, for that matter, what failed. Gompertz goes on to say:

> Failure is subjective, marginal, and mercurial. For years Monet, Manet, and Cézanne had their paintings rejected by the all-powerful Salon in Paris. All three artists were considered failures. But within a few years, they were hailed as visionary pioneers whose paintings went on to be considered some of the most important works of art produced in the modern period. Who, then, in hindsight, failed? It would appear the Salon, not the artists.[3]

---

3. Gompertz, *Think Like an Artist*, 47.

Thank goodness Renoir didn't hang up his painting jacket after the first rejection, let alone a rejection from the Salon. Sometimes, you must make your own Salon—just as Renoir and his contemporaries did. Many artists who have been shut out of mainstream venues have gone on to create totally new—and very profitable—ventures.

That is why it's important to remember that failure is part of the creative process. But it doesn't mean it's the end of the road.

The More You Fail, the More You Succeed

Creativity-related failure is often unclear, inexact, and temporary. But this does not mean much to you if the small business you created just declared bankruptcy. It hurts. It hurts bad. There seems to be no purpose to it. It feels unchangeable. The business indeed may not survive, but you will, and the so-called business failure is the reason why. The experience of failure is an essential part of the creative process, and there is no way of getting around it. Alberto Giacometti, the painter and sculptor, knew this feeling intimately. He said, "The more you fail, the more you succeed. It is only when everything is lost and—instead of giving up—you go on, that you experience the momentary prospect of some slight progress. Suddenly you have the feeling—be it an illusion or not—that something new has opened up."[4]

Giacometti knew, as do all artists, that one must aim for perfection even though perfection is unobtainable. Plato states in his *Theory of Forms* that perfection lives only in the realm of thought. There exists only one of every idea and the rest are just copies. The more you accept that nothing can be as perfect as you imagined in your mind, the better

4. Alberto Giacometti, quoted in Michael Kimmelman, "The Complexities of Seeing," review of *The Complexities of Seeing* by David Sylvester, *The New York Times*, 1996.

you will be at accepting the imperfections and failures that make up your creative life. The most important thing to remember is to never give up.

Never Give Up

Let's go back to Renoir. Not only did he not give up after his rejections, but he also didn't let physical ailments slow him down. He developed rheumatoid arthritis when he was in his forties. But he kept on painting to the very end, at seventy-nine years old. Although there was, at the time, no treatment for arthritis, he did his very best work at the end of his life in a wheelchair with paintbrushes strapped to his hand. The need to create was greater than the aches in his body!

The Evaluation Archetype: Analyst

Many times, the right idea combination takes time to present itself. The solution is not clear—sometimes you require an objective opinion. You need an Analyst. That is why the archetype for evaluation requires you to behave like an analyst.

In the realm of psychology, therapists listen to their patients talk and share their feelings and thoughts. The job of the analyst isn't to agree with the patient; it's not to cheerlead or to admonish and judge. Ideally, an analyst helps their patient take an inventory of their thoughts, actions, feelings, and behaviors and helps them find the underlying cause of their behavior and what is working for them and what is not. A common refrain in behavioral therapy is, "How is that working for you?" If a patient admits to drinking every day, for example, the analyst will not say something like, "Don't do that. You need to stop." Nor will they judge the patient as morally weak or physically inferior for not being able to resist alcohol. Rather, they will try to help their patient *analyze* their current condition. What impact is it having on their life? Relationships? Work? And chances are that during the analysis the patient will find that they do reap some benefits from the behavior—they might feel numb, less stressed out, more relaxed or at ease. Which will lead the analyst to ask, "Why do you need to feel this way? What is going on that makes you feel stressed and uneasy?" By asking questions and answering them, without judgment, the analyst and patient can understand the situation better—why the patient feels the need to drink excessively, for example, or what contributing factors at home or work or from their past might need to be addressed. At the heart of analysis is curiosity.

In his eponymous Apple TV show, the character Ted Lasso is a soccer coach who is the butt of everyone's jokes. No one thinks he can lead his team, not even his boss, who hired him hoping he would drive her ex-husband's team into the ground. During a pivotal scene in a bar, Ted Lasso stands up in front of his boss, her ex-husband, and the entire bar and aims a dart at a dartboard, and says, "Guys have underestimated me my entire life and for years I never understood why—it used to really bother me. Then one day I was driving my little boy to school, and I saw a quote by Walt Whitman. It was painted on the wall and it said, 'Be curious, not judgmental.' I like that." Ted threw the dart and won, but more important, he showed everyone around him what he was all about. Instead of counting him out, people would be better off if they got to know him. As the show progresses, everyone does—including himself. By working with an "analyst," or therapist, Ted even learns to not judge himself too harshly.

The reality is that judgment paralyzes us. It turns "mistakes" into "failures." It makes "I did this one thing wrong" into "I am a horrible person with no redeeming qualities." Curiosity, on the other hand, makes us investigators. It invites us to ask questions. It compels us to look for "what is working" rather than what is not. It asks us to look for more answers and solutions, rather than problems.

Curiosity with Patience

Using curiosity to find solutions is easier said than done. Again, the word "patience" comes up. This time, however, it is closely linked to curiosity. Often these insights don't reveal themselves instantly. One must be patient while digging deeper and sifting through all the possibilities.

Playfulness

If you have ever walked into a kindergarten classroom or the office of a child psychologist, you will find all kinds of toys to play with. Children learn by playing, and analysts learn about their patients by observing them at play. As an Analyst, you need to observe the play and be willing to sort things out—what works and what doesn't. Stack the proverbial Legos. Decorate the Barbie Dreamhouse. Draw a picture of a pirate ship with crayons and markers. Create a pretend battle while hiding behind a cardboard box. When we were children, ideas came easily. One child would initiate an idea, and another would add a new rule or imagine a new scenario. Soon you weren't just sitting in a cardboard box—you were sailing across the ocean, on your way to discover new lands and fend off pirates. No one was judging you; no one was criticizing. It was there you figured out what "worked." You figured out what ideas you absolutely loved and were ready to run with and which ones you wanted to abandon. Similarly, the Analyst looks and waits for the right idea combinations to fall in love with and knows when they have found them. These combinations usually come from ideas that:

- Build on previous ideas that have worked but could use improvement
- Arouse your curiosity and are captivating
- Contain beautiful designs that you can fall in love with
- Express simplicity (getting down to the core), efficiency (doing the most with the least), and elegance (beauty, precision, refinement)

Persistence

The Analyst doesn't give up. As Steven Pressfield says in *The War of Art*, "The professional self-validates. She is tough-minded. In the face of indifference or adulation, she assesses her stuff coldly and objectively. Where it fell short, she'll improve it. Where it triumphed, she'll make it better still. She'll work harder. She'll be back tomorrow."[5]

Creativity Myth: You Should Not Have a Plan B

I know many people who, when pursuing their craft or their profession, boldly profess, "The reason I am so successful is I didn't have a plan B. I just went for it." I disagree. I think there comes a time in every creative life when one has to assess the futility of the enterprise. Sometimes it makes sense to abandon the proverbial pirate ship and start over, especially if it is sinking. There are no guarantees in life. Nothing is a "sure thing," and it just makes sense to have a backup plan, better known as a plan B. I don't think of the plan B, though, in the way most others might. I hear parents who send their kids off to art school and whisper under their breath, "I hope they have a plan B—like to be an engineer

5. Steven Pressfield, *The War of Art: Break Through the Blocks and Win Your Inner Creative Battles* (Black Irish Entertainment, 2002), 79.

or a surgeon." What I hear them saying is, "I want my kid to be able to feed themselves, support themselves, have a good education so they are set up for success in life." It's scary for parents to send their children off to school, cross their fingers, and hope for the best. I think of a plan B as simply the road that diverged in the woods. Whichever direction their kids choose, both roads are taking them to the same destination—life as a fully human person who eats, breathes, dreams, lives, and loves. But the path might be different from the one they set off on.

Will Gompertz believes every innovative person—whether an entrepreneur, scientist, or artist—has one surprising common trait. In *Think Like an Artist*, he argues:

> Their success is very often down to Plan B. That is, the thing they originally set out to do has morphed along the way into something different. Shakespeare was an actor who became a playwright. The Rolling Stones were an R&B cover band until Mick Jagger and Keith Richards started writing their own songs. Leonardo da Vinci marketed himself as an armaments designer, and so on. The list of Plan Bs is long and illustrious. And instructive.[6]

I have had the opportunity to have creative failures (and thankfully plan Bs) in all the disciplines I have been involved in, whether in the operating room, in companies I've built and run, or in my art studios. Plan Bs are not compromises. They are something equally as exciting or intriguing as your plan A. I wouldn't be here today without my plan Bs.

Because sometimes you don't know if plan A is even right for you unless you actually implement your ideas. Implementation is key to discovery, and that's where we are headed in the next chapter.

---

6. Gompertz, *Think Like an Artist*, 62.

CASE STUDY

Evaluation in Action: Evaluating Healthcare Models and Balancing Innovation with Patient Needs

In his 2009 best-selling book, *The Big Leap*, Gay Hendricks writes about the concept of working within one's "zone of genius," which he defines as using all of your natural talents and doing what you enjoy—and what you are excellent at. You may be "excellent" at a lot of activities, but you may not be a natural at them or enjoy them. In other words, it's a struggle. Operating in your zone of genius is what you have spent years preparing for.

Most of us, however, don't recognize or give enough time to our "zones of genius" because we are often preoccupied with three other zones, which Hendricks also writes about. They are:

- The zone of incompetence: In this zone, you engage in something you are simply not good at (and haven't spent ample time preparing for or given much thought to).
- The zone of competence: Here you can get the job done, but no better than the next person. (For example, I may be good at bookkeeping, but it might not be the best use of my time, and I would probably be better off hiring someone to do it for me.)
- The zone of excellence: In this zone, you are doing something you are very, very good at compared to most people. (Most of us have several of these areas, but unfortunately, we aren't great at prioritizing, so some of these abilities lie dormant for years.)

The reality is that most of us don't struggle much with the first two zones. Where we get into real trouble is when we allow our zone of excellence, or what I like to call our "expert zone," to get in the way of our genius zone, or what Hendricks refers to as "our calling."

Most of us spend far too much time in our competence and excellence zones. They are safe and comfortable and don't require much risk. Many of us spend a lot of time doing something that we're "good at" but don't love and don't ever reach flow in, something that doesn't drastically change the outcomes of our daily life.

Hendricks argues that our problem is not that we lack expertise in one given thing but rather that we are *too good or "excellent" at too many things*. And it's robbing us of the time, space, and energy to focus on one thing we could be "genius" at. It's a bit like analysis paralysis—when you know way too much about too much, so you can't choose anything. The best way to find your own genius zone is to discover what makes you unique and where you can make the biggest impact using it.

Typically, the areas where our "genius" lies also coincide with things we love—or are extremely passionate about. If you suspect that you may be simply going through the motions and working in your zone of competence or your zone of excellence rather than your zone of genius, ask yourself the following questions:

- *Do I love what I am doing?*
- *Do I serve others while I am doing it? Does doing this thing make me feel more human and alive?*
- *Am I doing what I most excel at and what no one else around me seems to know better or do better at? (Remember, you may have many areas you are excellent at—but be honest, what are you the best at? What is there no one else can do?)*
- *Do I feel like I am creatively engaged when I am doing this thing?*
- *Does time pass quickly when I am doing it?*

Chances are, if the answer is no to any of these questions, you are working from a zone of competence or zone of excellence. To find your zone of genius, it is best to combine zones of excellence. Consider your unique abilities and combine them. For example, even before reading Hendricks's book, I had recognized that large hospitals were basically working from their zones of competence, and in many cases incompetence, but never excellence and genius. If I wanted to really make a change in the healthcare world, I would have to work from my zone of genius—where my purpose, flow, knowledge, creativity, and service to others all worked together. When I was evaluating my areas of expertise as well as the areas of healthcare that needed improvement, I realized I had found my zone of genius. I knew healthcare, I knew my industry inside and out, I was passionate about improving it, and I loved what I was doing. It all just "flowed" together.

Connecting the Dots

Evaluation comes down to finding the right dots and then connecting them most efficiently. Our strategy at HCDS was to bring affordability, constant quality, and convenient access to healthcare. These were the main dots we needed to connect. It was a formidable challenge. We were essentially trying to overhaul how medicine had been delivered to patients for the better part of two hundred years in this country. Trying to go from incompetent/competent–level care to excellent/genius–level care was indeed what Hendricks calls a "Big Leap." I wanted to provide not just competent care but excellent or genius care. People need services that are closer to their home. They don't want to go to some huge, centralized hospital that's full of complexity, where they can't even park their car. I also wanted to make sure we were sending patients home the same day. We wanted to reduce their bills, rates of infection, and inconvenience. It was never about providing just competent care. I wanted excellent, or genius-level, care, which meant thinking outside the box.

This is where the evaluation stage came in handy. The main Jobs to Be Done in this stage are to *connect* and combine ideas, then *choose* the best combination. These are precisely the same steps Hendricks advises when trying to assess your own zone of genius. You list all the areas where you are competent and work well, and then isolate one or two and combine them to produce your zone of genius. At HCDS, we first used different business models and emerging technologies to connect these dots innovatively. Then we limited ourselves to musculoskeletal care. We selected a field of expertise we knew we could execute with excellence and ran with it. Sure, we could have tried to tackle *all* of healthcare, but instead we decided to combine the areas of our individual zones of excellence, in order to arrive at our collective zone of genius. I combined my expertise in surgery and years of working in hospitals into one area—a healthcare delivery company in my region.

If you walked into one of our clinics with, for example, a knee problem, all the services you might need could be obtained at the same easy-to-access outpatient site: examination, imaging, possible surgery, and rehabilitation. All of this would be available at a location that was friendly and convenient for the patient and their family—one-stop shopping!

We were fifteen years into the making of HCDS when the book *The Medici Effect* came out in 2004 and twenty years in when *The Big Leap* came out in 2009, and it was only after researching *this book* that I learned about them! Nevertheless, I was using the principles of the Medici Effect and the zone of genius when I was developing the innovations and systems we used at HCDS. Namely, the intersection of different fields (discipline, cultures) both within and outside healthcare was responsible for an explosion of ideas. HCDS was driven by the intersection of different fields within my zones of excellence.

Roadblocks at HCDS

In order to find creative ideas at the intersection of fields, we needed to break through these "chains of associations" Frans Johansson mentions above. I like to think of these chains as mental roadblocks. Many physicians and administrators held certain beliefs based on their past experiences. They didn't question why or how we did things. Over the years, I heard many concerns, such as "sports medicine is only for the young and athletic." People like Dr. Robert Leach had significantly furthered the understanding of the special needs of the athlete, and the newer surgical techniques were meant to be used on athletes—professional, college, and maybe high school. Everyone else—the athlete's parents, let alone their grandparents, or the average jogger, weekend tennis player, recreational basketball player, or Wednesday night bowling leaguer—should be realistic when it came to expecting treatment for their injuries or ailments. The conventional medical advice at the time was always something along the lines of "Perhaps see a physical therapist for some home exercise instruction." Or "Buy a knee wrap at a local drugstore." Or "For goodness' sake, give away those skis!" Or "You can forget basketball, softball, and baseball! You're too old for that!" All terrible advice, we know now. A lifetime of daily activity and exercise is key to overall health and longevity. But for far too long, people suffered with injuries or pain and just gave up altogether.

In fact, up until a few decades ago, joint replacement was seen only as a last-ditch effort for the elderly. I had so many patients who said their husbands or wives were tired of seeing them limping and hearing them moaning in pain at night. They blamed it all on some early injury—high school football or years on the dance floor. They took the NSAIDs until their stomachs churned, and they had their knees "scoped." They couldn't do the recommended physical therapy exercises because they hurt too much. Their parents, who were in their eighties, had similar problems and had knee replacements and were now walking better than them. When they asked their surgeons about a knee replacement, they were told they had to wait until they were much older because it would just get worn down and they'd need another one. The only option was to suffer in pain. It was a completely inexcusable response, and yet for decades so many people suffered.

Another roadblock was the belief that all orthopedic surgery had to be inpatient—at least overnight, if not for days or weeks.

Another roadblock was hospital executives' long-held belief that only doctors (MD/DO) should see patients, dictate medical records, or be part of a surgical team. The use of physician's assistants (PAs) and nurse practitioners (NPs) was discouraged because healthcare executives thought that their abilities were restricted and that they needed to be closely monitored by physicians. The thinking was that "if they want to be doctors, they should go to medical school." This attitude often prevailed despite the fact that there were physician shortages, that training programs for PAs and NPs were of top quality, and that patients loved both them and their bedside manner. Removing this barrier was key to seamlessly integrating care and allowed everyone to be on the same page.

Another, thankfully now outdated, belief was that "orthopedic surgery is a man's world." It was a highly sexist and misogynistic field. The orthopedic surgeons of the past put people in full body casts, hammered large rods down broken thigh bones, and talked about sports both with each other and, as often as they could, with their patients. You might hear an old-school orthopedist say, "Girls might make good internists, but they would not be happy in the orthopedic men's club." Of course, we've come a long way in orthopedics—first, by not calling female physicians "girls," and second, by not excluding genders from practicing.

Smashing Through Roadblocks

By creating XF teams at HCDS, where staff members' zones of genius intersect with each other's fields and subfields, we were able to smash through barricades that would otherwise have blocked progress, such as conventional thinking regarding where operations could be performed, how long patients needed to recover, the location of the buildings, who had access to the records, and even who was eligible to receive care. Minimally invasive knee ligament repair was now possible for the fifty-five-year-old weekend warrior. And it was certainly a possibility for a forty-two-year-old wrestling coach in need of a joint replacement. With the proper post-op teaching and post-op planning, even a knee replacement patient might go home the same day as surgery. The XF teams produced the environment for divergent thinking needed for powerful new ideas. And these were ideas that led to innovations in patient care.

Given the opportunity, NPs and PAs became significant parts of the patient care team. They were welcomed by patients and eventually by doctors. It took a few years, but eventually a female orthopedic surgeon joined the HCDS medical staff. These victories were often accompanied by substantial battles (which I will detail in chapter 8). There were those in the general hospital community, insurance world, and medical community who were threatened by, and as a result sought to find fault with, the type of breakthrough innovation that we were achieving. But these challenges never dissuaded us. If we had focused on the roadblocks, we never would have progressed further. Sometimes you have to ignore "no" and "this is the way it's always been done" in order to proceed. Sometimes you have to break the rules—written or unwritten—to truly innovate.

Summary: Living at the HCDS Intersections

What actually happened at HCDS when the roadblocks were pushed aside? In other words, how did the intersection of fields deliver the creative ideas?

What often happened was that a combination of two or more different ideas collided in an unplanned manner. For example, what might happen to a fifty-five-year-old patient who tore his cruciate ligament in his knee. The protocol at the time was, once the knee swelling subsided, to have him do some exercises, expect his knee to give out at times, and give up tennis. Surgery was never called for or conducted on middle-aged individuals—it was saved for athletes and much younger patients. But we had the intersection of me and my zone of excellence—perfecting knee ligament repairs with arthroscopic techniques—a physical therapist, Gary, who was excellent at early mobilization of the knee with protective bracing immediately after surgery; and a cooperative middle-aged participant, Gerry, who was willing to try something new and was willing to do the work to make sure he healed just as well as if he were a running back at Lehigh University.

Gary and I had helped a number of college athletes return successfully to contact sports. We felt that the combination of minimally invasive arthroscopic surgery and aggressive, but protected, rehabilitation might work for the older individual as well. Gerry understood the possibilities for failure but was emphatic that we give it a try. We all worked *together* to fix Gerry's ligament. Gerry went back to tennis and we started fixing others like him—as did the rest of the country.[7]

We were now ready for implementation.

---

7. Names have been changed to protect the privacy of patients.

Jump-Start Your Creativity

Writing prompts for your journal:

- Pull out your mind map. Are there any related ideas you could combine to make something new? Are there any unrelated ideas that you could combine?
- Make a list of all the ideas you have gathered recently. Which one is the best, in your opinion? Which one do you want to run with? Or is there one you would love to spend more time working on? Which one excites and energizes you?
- How do you cope with mistakes or perceived failures? Is this an area you can reframe and shift your thinking on?
- What was something in your past that you considered a "failure" but that turned out to be a positive or educational experience?
- Consider your own zones of competence, incompetence, excellence, and genius. Divide a sheet of paper into four columns, one for each zone. Then think about all the activities you've completed over the last week and write each down in the column corresponding to its zone. Are there activities in your zones of incompetence and competence that you could outsource in order to clear the way for "excellence" and "genius"?
- What activities do you most love to do? What could you do for hours at a time without getting bored? What makes you feel most alive and human?
- Which of your zones of excellence could you combine into zones of genius? To do this, consider your unique abilities and combine them. I find Venn diagrams helpful for this. (For example, I combined arthroscopic surgery with my systems

thinking and design thinking to produce HCDS.) Could you create a couple of your own Venn diagrams to help you find your zone of genius?

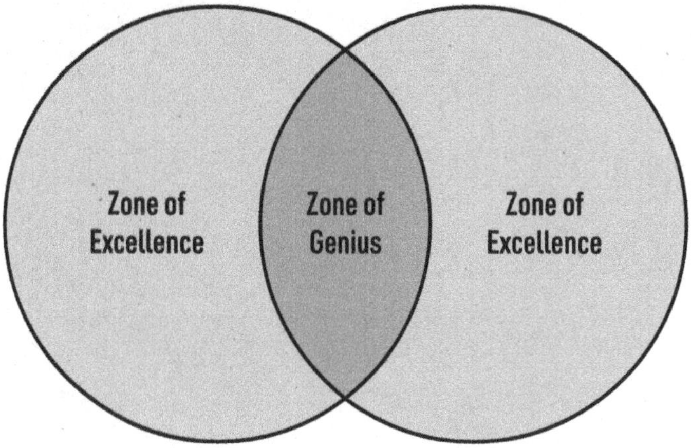

CHAPTER 8

Stage 5: Implementation

In 1975, an art historian and museum director at the Basilica di San Lorenzo, the official church of the Medici family, made an astonishing discovery when he spotted a trapdoor below a wardrobe. The trapdoor opened into a narrow room measuring eleven by thirty-three feet, which contained dozens of drawings. Some of these drawings looked startlingly familiar. Although none of the sketches were signed, they were very similar to the naked forms and sculptures throughout Florence and Italy that were attributed to Michelangelo. Since the Medici were Michelangelo's patron, it is more than likely that this room was indeed a workshop of sorts for the master and his contemporaries.

Not far from San Lorenzo stands the Florentine art workshop Bottega dell'Opera del Duomo. Founded in 1296, it is where Michelangelo worked on his *David*. Before that, it is where he served as an apprentice in the workshop of Domenico Ghirlandaio, while living in the Medici Palace and studying in the Medici sculpture garden. It was in this workshop and the Medici Palace, surrounded by sculptures and the works of earlier Renaissance artists, that Michelangelo learned the art of sketching, sculpture, and fresco painting. Even though some historians have argued that Michelangelo was "gifted" from birth or had "divine" artistic talents, this doesn't tell the whole story. Michelangelo was *trained* and he was an apprentice—who spent many hours, days, and years in workshops and rooms sketching, drawing, and sculpting. In other words, working. Hence the word "work" in workshop.

I have named my studio and workshop Atelier Lucca, with *atelier* being the French word for workshop. Many artists and, most commonly, fashion designers call the spaces they work in *ateliers*. We named our sculpture studio and gardens Atelier Lucca because we envisioned a place where artists, sculptors, horticulturalists, landscape architects, and even writers could come and wrestle with their creative ideas together.

The term "workshop" doesn't just refer to the physical space itself. If you happen to Google art classes or programs in your local area, that word will come up frequently. Writers attend "writers' workshops" to "workshop" (also used as a verb) the latest drafts of their poems, memoirs, or novels. Potters, photographers, and painters attend workshops where they can practice their crafts with like-minded individuals. Carpenters, mechanics, and DIYers of all kinds also have workshops where they tinker, work out their ideas, fix, build, and create. I also have a workshop, where I sculpt and paint and try out and finalize my ideas with a team of other sculptors and artists. I love how the word "work" is juxtaposed with the word "shop"—two unlikely words when thinking of creativity.

Most people don't immediately think of creativity as "work." Creativity is often relegated to the dismissive term "hobby." Writers, poets, painters, photographers, singers, dancers, innovators, inventors, and tinkerers of all kinds are said to be dabbling in a "hobby" when they create—until, of course, they start making money or gain recognition for their work. But were they any less creative when they were working in the shadows and for no pay? I don't think so. And the word "shop" is curious too. When we think of a shop, we think of shopping, consuming, and selling, not creating. But inherent in the word "shop" is the notion of an audience, a buyer, a person to make the art or item for. When we "workshop" something, what we are doing is *making something for someone*, that someone being an end user, consumer, purveyor, or appreciator.

To create means to work on something for someone else—it is the ultimate human activity that brings us in full communion with ourselves, as workers, and others. It allows us to be a person who contributes in some way to others' lives. In other words, in this last stage of the creative process, implementation, we get out of our own heads and *head* into the workshop. We start to execute. After preparation, incubation, insight, and evaluation, the rubber is about to meet the road. Idea combinations must transform into reality. We must start making the thing—with a person, a buyer, an audience member, collector, or some other person in mind.

Michelangelo created his works for popes and patrons. His art, to this day, is admired by millions. John Lennon wrote music and recorded it in studios with his friends Paul, George, and Ringo before releasing it to millions of fans who have spanned decades. What makes the implementation stage so interesting—and complicated—is that we take the ideas that have been (for the most part) existing only in our heads and on sticky notes and start painting the proverbial walls. We start chiseling the marble. We start singing and recording. We sit in front of our computer and we begin typing our book. We share the pages with others for evaluation and feedback. We go back to the computer and make the necessary changes. We check out what works and what doesn't. We keep doing this over and over, until we are satisfied. At the end of this stage, we will have a physical product of some kind, whether it's just a prototype or the final version. In this stage we work to bring our ethereal ideas into the physical realm.

A Word on Originality

It is important to remember this: while we are busy manifesting in the physical world, we don't have to produce something completely original. Nothing comes from nowhere. All creative work builds on what came before—nothing is completely original. The French writer André Gide wrote, "Everything that needs to be said has already been said. But since no one was listening, everything must be said again."

We can stop trying to create something out of thin air. Every new idea is a combination of previous old ideas. And the latter is a result of our experiences. Our experiences are a result of what we allow to enter our lives—that is, the things that we fall in love with.

I love the concept of stone-wall building. I see myself as somebody who can pick out the really unique stones and knows how to best join them together. I'm good at figuring out how to stabilize the stones so they won't fall. I fuss and gripe as I pick them out, especially the heavy ones. The one thing I know for sure is that I can assemble the stones but I can't make them. I didn't "invent" the rocks or construct them, but I can gather and arrange them in a way that is new to me, to others. That is what all of creativity is. It's gathering rocks that already exist and putting them in a new formation.

Doing the Work and Making the Space for It

Let me caution you: the implementation stage is often the one that is the hardest and takes the most time. It is indeed "work." And often, implementation requires a workshop—a place for you to go and create, make, play, iterate, build upon, start over, try out with peers or reviewers, and keep at it. This space doesn't need to be fancy. We don't need the funding of SpaceX when we start. I know podcasters who launched their million-dollar-idea podcast from their closets. They closed the door and hooked up a microphone and that is all they needed. Writers need only, as Virginia Woolf advised, "a room of one's own"—a quiet space (if that is how they work best) to retreat to where they can write for a half hour, an hour, or six.

We don't all have patrons like Michelangelo did or the sculpture gardens of the Medici Palace from which to draw our inspiration. But most of us have access to a public library, local free museums, park spaces, and warm, cozy coffee shops—most of which have Wi-Fi these days. We can all make do. I have Atelier Lucca right on my home's property, so I only have to walk across the garden to start working. Most of us can find a space, no matter how small, for our creative endeavors. Because if you're about to "make" something, you need a space to do so. Don't have a garage? What about a basement? No basement? Can you convert a room or a closet? Find a space to work in, and then get to it.

Progress over Perfection—and a Sense of Humor

In this stage the old adage about seeking "progress over perfection" holds true. Trying a lot of stuff comes down to testing your ideas—that is, your solutions. It's a matter of being flexible enough to alter your course after you have received some tough feedback. This is when burnout can sneak in, especially if you try to act as a stickler for perfection. You must be okay with things turning out messy. Julia Child burned a lot of chicken before she ever became a world-renowned chef, TV personality, and author. She spent hours toiling in her own workshop—a kitchen she expertly designed herself with all of her tools, pans, and ingredients efficiently laid out for her use. Whenever she was cooking on live TV and took a misstep, she would often laugh and run with her mistakes, even turning some of them into beloved recipes and moments on television. Who can forget Dan Aykroyd's famous impression of her saying, "I cut the dickens out of my finger!" on *SNL*, which was inspired by a time when the famous chef cut herself before going live on the air. Child took Aykroyd's impersonation on the chin and was able to laugh at herself. In one episode of her show, she paused her cooking and advised her audience to not "be afraid of failure in the kitchen." Cooking, she said, is "one failure after another."

"It's how we learn," she advised. She couldn't have been more right.

Don't Rush It, and Trust That It's Worth It

The implementation effort is always a battle that takes work, and often money. But it also takes time—weeks, months, and for me, years. Make sure enough time is part of your execution plan.

It's often in this stage that we may ask ourselves, *Is this creativity thing really worth it?* Tolstoy took ten years to write *War and Peace*, Margaret Mitchell took ten years to write *Gone with the Wind*, J. R. R. Tolkien took seventeen years to write *The Lord of the Rings*, and Michael Crichton took twenty years to write *Sphere*. Great works take time. It's hard to see the payoff amid the struggle, but it will arrive. It's why we keep reading and keep looking for inspiration outside ourselves, as well as some hints from those who have gone before us that the time will come when it will be done. But how will you know? you ask. You'll feel it in your heart. You will know it's time to be done. Sometimes, it's because you know you simply can't work on it one more day. That is usually a sign. And once it's released into the world, you will feel that indescribable sense of completion that comes only from creating something and seeing it through to the end. You will have made your mark, left your imprint, however small or large, on the human journey that is uniquely yours, as insane as it might be.

JTBD 1: Make the Work

Although ideas and their connections are at the center of creativity, at some point we must go from idea combinations to reality. In other words, we must make something that has a physical form. As children we may have played with Legos or blocks or built models—cars, ships, trains, dollhouses—to bring our imaginations to life. When we are in the creative process of implementation, we must "make something."

This helps us further the process that combines ideas and builds upon what appears to work. This is a process that I call "thinkering."

Thinkering: Thinking with Our Hands

I first came across the term "thinkering" when reading Michael Ondaatje's wonderful novel *The English Patient*. Kip, a character in the book, muses, "The word should be thinkering," as he observes a "woman thinking" while she is moving her hands.[1] She is the nurse who was in the villa with him, a bomb expert. With the word "thinkering," Kip expresses the act of creating and understanding concepts in the mind while physically working with one's hands. Idea production

1. Michael Ondaatje, *The English Patient* (Vintage International, 1993), 125.

can happen while working with your hands. They work together. This concept of thinkering, a combination of thinking and tinkering, highlights three specific areas. First, it focuses on the connection between the physical and the mental. It emphasizes that practical hands-on engagement with the world, like Kip's meticulous work of diffusing bombs, is a form of deep thought and comprehension, rather than just mindless labor. Second, thinkering is a mode of understanding. It suggests that some forms of knowledge and emotional process can be achieved only through physical action and interaction with objects and one's environments. Third, thinkering is healing. This is important too. The characters in the ruined villa are all damaged. They are people trying to heal themselves and each other. Because the villa's inhabitants use the act of thinkering to process their lives, memories, and immediate surroundings, the villa itself becomes a pathway to recovery and finding meaning amid the chaos of war. Ultimately, the term "thinkering" encapsulates a core theme of the novel: the interplay between the internal world of memory and identity and the external world of physical objects and actions.

Since the publication of this novel, the term "thinkering" has come to mean thinking while one tinkers or uses their hands. To think means to use the brain to create and understand a concept, and to tinker means to make small physical changes to something to improve it or to play around with things and ideas, trying to see what happens. Thinkering, then, is *an active form of thinking*. We think about an idea, a possible solution, by tinkering with an item that is associated with the problem we are trying to solve. In other words, we try to solve the problem by doing stuff rather than just sitting and staring at it.

According to the neuroscience, when we learn by making things with our hands, we create new neural connections, which in turn create new ideas. This ability for the neural networks to form new connections—essentially rewire themselves—is known as neuroplasticity. Recent research suggests that this type of hands-on work might even contribute to our happiness and overall well-being. In other words, making or thinkering makes us better humans. In Dr. Kelly Lambert's book *Lifting Depression: A Neuroscientist's Hands-On Approach to Activating Your Brain's Healing Power*, she argues that using our hands is the best way to reach overall well-being. Making things helps us develop self-esteem, purpose, and a sense of personal autonomy and freedom. It also makes us smarter and even more creative the more we do it. Whether we are crocheting a stuffed animal for a friend, cooking a homemade meal for our family, digging in the garden, or tinkering with a broken pipe, we're actually bathing our brain in a wash of chemicals that make us feel better—dopamine, serotonin, and oxytocin. Whenever we are engaging in the creative process using our hands, our brains literally become optimized to learn, plan, make choices, and iterate even faster. Dr. Lambert writes,

> Our hands play a crucial role when it comes to effort-driven rewards. From an evolutionary perspective, it is easy to see why they have always been so critical to our survival: they allow us to gain control of our environment. In fact, an essential premise of the proposed effort-driven-rewards theory is that movement—and especially hand movements that lead to desired outcomes—plays a key role in both preventing the onset of and building resilience against depression and other emotional disorders.[2]

This makes a lot of sense to me. I can feel my mood drift and change if I haven't been able to draw or sculpt. And we need only look

---

2. Kelly Lambert, *Lifting Depression: A Neuroscientist's Hands-On Approach to Activating Your Brain's Healing Power* (Basic Books, 2008). Excerpt printed in *Scientific American Mind*, September 2008, 34.

at the world around us to see how detrimental not creating or playing is. Today, kids and teens are reporting record levels of depression and anxiety—as well as an addiction to their phones and social media. With their reduced amount of social connection, play, tinkering, thinkering, and drawing, it's no wonder they are so unhappy. There was a time when kids used to tinker all the time, especially with crayons. Now they are given phones, video game consoles, and iPads and sent on their way. As adults, we also don't engage in tinkering nearly enough. We are often afraid to take risks, try something new, and stumble onto something we did not previously know. But these are important elements of creativity—and our happiness and well-being.

Drawing and the Implementation Stage

It's best not to overthink thinkering. You don't have to build a full prototype. Drawing or sketching is the fastest and easiest way to externalize an idea. You don't have to be an artist. You just have to doodle! Drawing can help make the entire creative process more efficient and effective—especially the implementation stage. It is, as Virginia Woolf put it, a way "one could catch [one's thoughts] before they became 'works of art' . . . Catch them hot and sudden as they rise in the mind."

Matisse called it the "active thinking process." This includes drawings or diagrams for initial exploration and experimentation, followed by drawings for development and definition.

Drawing is a vehicle for expressing and recording ideas. The English artist Grayson Perry argues, "We don't have a USB port in our head and drawing is the most direct way we have of expressing our visual imagination to the outside world." Drawing provides a vehicle for speed in capturing these ideas quickly and externalizing them. It also provides a vehicle for brainstorming where many ideas are proposed and discarded to get to one that is suitable. Drawing provides a vehicle for connecting ideas during the incubation (subconscious) stage; it allows us to connect the dots. It also provides a vehicle for advancing ideas to development and definition—the implementation stage.

Gathering the Materials and Resources

At some point during the implementation stage, you need to create the final product. Once the prototype, the first draft, the drawings, the renderings, and so on are completed, they must be turned into reality. You need to do the work. The manuscript has to be completed, edited, and packaged with a query letter to be shipped off to select agents. The final piece has to be created. The house has to be built. The ground must be broken and the foundation for the new hospital has to be poured. This is where the creation must come to life. The only way to do this is, simply, to do it. This may mean finding the right people, resources, or location. And then you must be ready to let it go. Which leads to the second JTBD in implementation.

JTBD 2: Put the Work Out There

This is sometimes the hardest part. After years of preparing, incubating, thinking, evaluating, and elaborating, you must let go of your creation. A mother must wave goodbye to her five-year-old and send them off to kindergarten. The babies we cared for and nourished, our creative pursuits, are ready to take on lives of their own. We need to release them.

This is hard because now the entire world will be able to see them. This can be pretty scary. You can bet that not everyone will fall in love like you have. Some may have nasty things to say. Again, I've been there. I remember that when I first set out to conduct surgeries that would send patients home within a day, people thought I was crazy. I had to stick to my guns. I knew where the critics were coming from (they wanted to maintain the status quo), but I knew I could do it safely, so I took the shot. And you can too. Now is the time to put your big boy/girl pants on and keep going. It's you and a true expression of your creativity.

Even the most famous creators have faced rejection, denouncement, or ridicule. Finishing the work and releasing it doesn't necessarily guarantee success—at least at first. J. K. Rowling, the author of the Harry Potter series, received multiple rejections after she sent out the draft of her first book. A low-level editor pulled her manuscript out of a slush pile that was likely headed for the trash. That one reader changed the trajectory of Rowling's career. She gave her a chance. And that's all she needed. After some time, audiences fell in love with her creation, and she went on to become one of the best-selling authors of all time. You only need one audience member to give you that start.

But a start is just *a start*. One person isn't enough. If you're going to release your work out into the world, you need to be prepared to present it to *the world*—that is, to more than one person. It's a lesson Henry Ford learned the hard way. Prior to founding the Ford Motor Company, Ford worked as a machinist, learning about the fabrication processes. He went on to work as an engineer at the Edison Illuminating Company, where he became the chief engineer. All those years served as preparation, incubation, insight, and evaluation stages as he worked on projects of his own, including building the prototype of the first internal combustion engines. In 1896, he built his first full vehicle, which he named the Quadricycle; it was the early prototype of the automobile. Once he felt he had something ready to release to the world, he quit his engineering job and started his own company, the Detroit Automobile Company. Ford focused entirely on the mechanics, rather than the business of marketing and sales, and his first product failed. With no one to buy his vehicle, he was forced to file for bankruptcy.

But he didn't let this dissuade him. He used the bankruptcy to start over with a clean slate, this time incorporating valuable information he had learned from his failures. Specifically, he hired business-savvy individuals to help him market and sell his creation.

How you convey the work to the outside world is important; sometimes it's as important as the work itself. Every book needs a well-designed book cover, an engaging title, and a plan to reach readers—through social media, blogs, and podcasts, as well as bookstore and library events. A product needs to be appropriately priced, packaged beautifully, and placed in optimal locations to catch a buyer's eye. In other words, thought needs to be given to how your creation is presented. Your product should be professional. You should be ready to talk about the work and to defend the work. You'll need to take some time to think through and anticipate questions that will be asked about the work. Ford's big mistake was he assumed that if he built it, they would come. And that's simply not the case. Yes, it's important to complete the process of building and making, but at some point, you also have to figure out the best way to get that creation into the hands of an audience.

Finally, it's when your work is most creative that someone out there will find it the most threatening—they will find fault with it, try to censure it, cast aspersions upon it, and denounce it. Be ready and be brave. There is no bigger target than a successful or daring person—especially one who pushes against the status quo.

A Word on Feedback

There is a difference between derision (usually a result of jealousy, fear, or lack of understanding) and good, constructive feedback. Feedback intends to make the work better; it is not meant to hurt or harm. Though it can hurt to hear negative feedback, it's important to discern its intention. Constructive feedback does just what it says—it constructs. It builds. It tells the creator how their work can be improved or enhanced. It points out blind spots that they may not be able to see because they are so close to the work.

When you receive feedback, try to depersonalize the process and remember that people are judging your work and not you. This is one of those "easier said than done" moments in life. When we pour our blood, sweat, and tears into something, it's easy to start blurring the lines of where you end and the creation begins. We can all become very attached to our own ideas. We can get our minds stuck on the way we think something should be and then resist others' feedback, especially when it requires us to completely redo something we already worked hard on.

It has often been hard for me to receive feedback and stay positive. There have been times when I have not even listened to the information being shared with me. The year before I became chief resident in Boston, I worked under one of Robert Leach's attending physicians. I was working in one of the busiest, most stressful inner-city hospitals in the country. On any particular evening, we saw all manner of injuries and illnesses. It was like walking into a war zone every night. Gunshot wounds, stabbings, major motor vehicle and motorcycle accidents—you name it, we saw it. It was not unlike the fast-paced scenes in the television drama *ER* that was popular in the nineties.

But, unlike in *ER*, my attending was no suave, charismatic, confident George Clooney. In fact, I thought the guy was a real pain in the ass. In my opinion, this man wasn't up for the challenge of working in a high-stakes ER. He was far too timid and didn't have the required intensity or focus to be in any ER, let alone one in the middle of inner-city Boston. And being a young, extremely confident surgeon, I basically told him as much one night when I said to him, "Please get back. I will handle this." I wasn't wrong. I knew he couldn't do what needed to be done for the young, dying patient on our operating room table. She had been wheeled in with two broken femurs after being thrown from a motorcycle. Nevertheless, looking back on it—as I do now with decades of experience under my belt—I realize I went too far. There was a better way to convey my message.

The next morning, Dr. Leach approached me and said, "I heard from my attending, Dr. Smith, last night. He was not happy at all with the way you handled yourself in the operating room. I want you to know that if this continues, you may have to repeat the year here." I was stunned. This was the first time I had received feedback like this, and I thought I was going to *die*. But instead of apologizing, I dug in. "You know, I'm the guy that handled that case," I responded. "Dr. Smith didn't even know how to do it. I don't care if he's the attending. I did that case. And that was a difficult case at two o'clock in the morning. It was a bilateral open femur fracture. I stepped right in. I took the junior residents with me, and we took care of it." Dr. Leach just gave me a look that said, "You're finished."

Later, I tracked down Dr. Leach and apologized. I realized I was way out of line. And he said something to me I will never forget. "Dr. Smith is an attending. You're not. He passed the boards. You didn't. You're not even chief resident."

I told him that I understood and apologized again and was careful from that point on to never behave the way I had in the OR that night. I know from experience that entitled arrogance and anger is a dangerous mixture.

Sure, we're all human and no one is perfect. There have been times when I have allowed my feelings and emotions to dominate. This never helps. Emotions must be kept under control. To combat these emotions, I must try to remember the importance of feedback for improvement.

I do my best to stay open-minded and avoid denial. Instead, I try to be a better listener. With time and practice, I have gotten better. And

I now ask other people for their opinions. It's only with these opinions that I can grow, learn, and move forward, and so can my work.

The Implementation Archetype: Builder

A Builder builds. A writer writes. A painter paints. A sculptor sculpts. A conductor conducts. A surgeon operates. A gardener gardens. A dancer dances.

A common conundrum many writers face is that they don't believe they can call themselves "a writer" unless they have been published. I have a friend who is a book editor, and she advises all the writers she works with, especially the unpublished ones, to call themselves writers *if in fact they do write.* That is the requirement of a writer, after all: to write. In the end, it is about what we do, and what we make of our ideas and talents. At some point, you have to do the work. Sometimes you have to swallow your pride, roll up your sleeves, and even get your hands dirty. Some of the work isn't glamorous. If you have ever been to the ballet and watched as a ballet dancer effortlessly glides across the stage, know that they spent thousands of hours in a studio practicing in order to appear weightless.

Sometimes the work is grueling, and sometimes it doesn't seem to make sense to an outsider. And that's okay. It's up to us creatives, not outsiders, to make sense of what we do. There is a wonderful story about Ulysses S. Grant that I love. Before he was the general who led the North in the Civil War, he was living in Saint Louis and struggling financially. One day an army friend of Grant's who knew him from his West Point days came upon him selling firewood by the road. He was shocked and said, "Great God, Grant, what are you doing?" And Grant's answer was simple: "I am solving the problem of poverty." Grant had a problem that needed a creative solution—he needed money to support himself—and so he grabbed an axe and got to work. In his mind, he was more than a logger; he was a creative problem solver. He was building his life, as he saw fit to do it, with the means he had.

The archetype for the implementation stage is the Builder. The Builder is out there doing the work, solving the problem at hand, and paying attention to the developing work so they can notice when new ideas and new problems arise. As you externalize the product and process, you need to keep in mind your original strategy and goals as the work proceeds.

The Value of Hard Work

At some point, there is no escaping the work that needs to be done. You have to show up at your desk, open Excel, and stare at the blank spreadsheet before you begin. You have to turn the lights on in the studio and start warming up. The Builder is a hard worker who gets up without telling anyone. They arrive early, stay late, and do more than is asked of them. They are like every company's star employee. They pay attention to the details and call out issues, instead of sweeping them under the carpet. They don't take shortcuts. They also finish what they start. They meet the deadlines they set for themselves and offer no excuses.

Enthusiastic

The Builder is energized and enthusiastic. They are in essence a cheerleader for themselves and their team. They are the ultimate promoter, defender, and champion of their work: their mantra is "We can do this!" They keep their team's spirits up—by keeping their own energy up. They go for walks, exercise, sleep, and eat well. They need their strength to finish what they started. Like a long-distance runner on the day of the marathon, they show up and are always ready to go the distance. They are fully charged, bouncing in place, ready to move. For them, it's go time.

Focused

The Builder is focused. They aren't easily distracted by the newest, shiniest object. They don't abandon their cause midway, even when things are difficult and feel overwhelming. They stay the course. They remember why they are here and what they set out to do. They keep their original strategy and plan in mind as the work proceeds, and they resist the temptation to get sidetracked.

Creativity Myth: Implementation Is Selling Out

Whenever we create something new and put it out in the world, we will be met with resistance. One of the worst things a creative can hear from a peer is the accusation that they are "selling out" by bringing their creation to light and selling it. This accusation is often directed at highly successful people. When Bob Dylan plugged his electric guitar into an amp at the Newport Folk Festival, people nearly rioted. Many told reporters they were disappointed in Dylan because, in their minds, he had sold himself out to the new world order of rock and roll. Dylan, on the other hand, wanted to try some new music that he felt called to create. When Hollywood actors who are known for their dramatic roles take on parts in comedies or action movies, some of their fans may cry, "Sellout!" There are plenty of actors, however, who truly care about all the roles they play—dramatic, comedic, or otherwise.

Christopher Reeve, a professionally trained actor, took a role in *Superman* that defined the rest of his career. He didn't care. He was proud of the work he did and loved showing up to the set each day and giving it his all. In contrast, he said, he believed costar Marlon Brando was the sellout. Not because Marlon Brando was a famous and lauded actor who succumbed to the $2 million paycheck for twelve lines (which he read instead of memorized) but because of how Brando behaved on set. In a *Late Night with David Letterman* appearance in 1982, Reeve came out and said that the reason he thought Marlon Brando "sold out" was that Brando "no longer cared." He was just doing it for the money. He showed up, read his lines (which were said to be taped on the chest of someone on set), took the money, and let the production give his name top billing to get fans in the seats. Reeve had a point.

Mind you, when we create anything and bring it to the world, it is perfectly okay to accept money for it. Receiving money for your work doesn't make it any less creative or worthy. You are no less a creative for creating something that can and will be enjoyed by others. In fact, the more people who enjoy your work, the better. But if you don't care about the work, the outcome, the creativity of it—as Brando didn't—then not only are you selling out, but you're also selling your soul, your humanity, as well. In a world of Brandos, be a Superman.

CASE STUDY

Implementation in Action: Building the Healthcare Company

In the mid-nineties, I was driving home from the state capital after a long day spent confronting state officials as well as attorneys from the local general hospitals. My hopes for getting a license for an outpatient surgery center appeared dim. I had entered the complicated intersection of state government and healthcare delivery politics, and I was taking quite a beating.

While I was sitting in my car, the president of one of the general hospitals called me and he dressed me down. He basically said I had no business trying to build more operating rooms—that was the hospital's job—and I should stick to being a surgeon. I had failed, but I was determined to try again. This intersection of different cultures (state government and healthcare delivery) called for building a team of different fields and disciplines. So that is what I did.

Over the years, I put together a diversified team of lawyers, architects, clinicians, and construction management experts. It took us three years, but we finally opened the first HCDS ambulatory surgery center. This team stayed together for several decades and ended up with more wins than losses. We all worked under one roof—if a lawyer needed to run something by any of the team members, the lawyer could find them just down the hall. If the architect needed answers about the OR construction, our clinical teams were readily available. Everyone worked in close proximity, and we managed every point of the patient's care within the walls of the HCDS buildings. All of our patient imaging and paper charts were moved across facilities as well—long before there was such a thing as Epic or other electronic health records.

We didn't just work in an isolated vacuum. I realized that if I really wanted to make an impact, I had to change how healthcare was delivered—and not just within my four walls. Eventually, once I got a lot smarter, I contracted with a lobbying firm that helped me steer through the state capital as well as Washington, DC. Even later, when we could afford it, HCDS started a political action fund to support candidates who might consider supporting the HCDS vision. It took some storytelling and convincing, but I found them.

The politics of the industry was an aspect I didn't particularly enjoy, but I knew it was essential to get this done. I had to implement and execute in the complex world of healthcare, where fairness was not always the standard of the day. In almost every field or industry, you will eventually find you are part of a larger ecosystem that is often fixed and set in its ways. It takes courage, strength, persistence, and a willingness to play the game or fight the battle if you want to go the distance.

The main lesson I learned when I lived at this intersection of healthcare and government was that I could never be absolutely sure where I was going until I got there. But I always had a plan and a purpose driving all my decisions and actions for the company. By taking one deliberate step at a time, I could trust that the process would lead to optimal results. In this case, by having our own operating rooms, we had achieved another milestone in our quest for vertical integration. Surgeons were more efficient, infection rates went down, and patients absolutely loved it!

Remaining Passionate

There were many institutions that opposed innovation at HCDS: large general hospital systems, large insurance carriers, and federal and state government agencies, just to name a few. Battles extended not just for weeks or months but quite often for years. Frequently we were in the win column, but many times they clobbered us. Our company's success was so important to me that I put on the hat of "Builder" during this time. Being hardworking, industrious, enthusiastic, focused, and passionate was key to sustaining my momentum, especially during the lean or tough years. For example, there were times when the general hospitals could not stop us from recruiting and building, so they tried to buy up our patient referral sources. The insurance companies paid us less than they paid the general hospitals even though our quality standards were published and among the highest in the country. The state agencies held up licenses we needed. There was no end to the roadblocks. But we kept going. To produce innovation within this intersection of opposition meant pushing past mistakes and disappointments and sticking to the strategy: lower cost, higher quality, and greater accessibility.

I believe the most critical factor that kept the HCDS cross-field teams going was *passion*. This passion kept us focused on our strategy even when failure seemed inevitable. Passion was the fuel that kept us going when others wanted to close us down—and said so publicly! How else could I have been able to do what I did? A mere orthopedic surgeon? Who did I think I was to start my own network? It was unbelievable, but I kept my head down and kept working.

The catalyst for this passion was the responses from the patients we treated and the universities and employers we served—the football players and women's soccer team at Lafayette College, the line workers at the Crayola factory, the financial executive who believed in us enough to have us replace his knee and funded our expansion. The more people we helped, the more lives we changed, the more urgently I felt my cause and purpose, and the more driven I was to continue and succeed.

This approach at the intersection of fields, disciplines, and cultures produced a diligence fueled by passion. It was the passion, not external expectations and rewards, that produced the creativity. Money is something good to have, but if you focus too much on money, you slow the creativity process for sure. We never lost sight of our cause and purpose—the patients. We wanted to change the lives of others, to make a real impact. And that was the fuel that kept us burning.

Escaping the Network

My teacher Clay Christensen had taught me to be aware of "value networks" when pursuing creativity. In the business world, a value network is a set of connections between organizations and/or individuals that benefit the entire group. The most important parts of a network are (1) customers, (2) services, (3) service providers, and (4) contracts that allow access to services. A value network is often defined as a network that allows members to both buy and sell products as well as share information. For example, social media is a value network. Christensen's work on value networks addressed the relations between a company, its suppliers, and the requirements posed by the customers, and how these interact when defining what represents value in a product.

Christensen pointed out that a business inside a value network will often have a much tougher time pursuing innovation than one that has managed to remain outside of one. (This can also be true for an individual.) The objective of a business inside a value network is to sell the most expensive products to their best customers. This usually results in an environment where innovation is difficult to produce. I had seen and studied this firsthand at Bethlehem Steel. In fact, Christensen often used Bethlehem Steel as an example of a victim of what he called "disruptive innovation." When competitors overseas were using advanced technologies and thus cutting costs on labor usage, Bethlehem Steel was slow to keep up. It couldn't compete against lower-cost, more efficiently made foreign steel.

Christensen also taught me that the only way to succeed in breaking away from an entrenched network is to stop relying on it. This was a main reason why HCDS broke away from the general hospital networks and eventually built its own specialty hospital with its own operating rooms.

But it was within this operating room environment that we encountered another established value network—the orthopedic implant industry. Implants were a significant part of our cost equation. Orthopedic implants are manufactured devices that can replace a joint, bone, or cartilage. The most common types of implants are screws, plates, and prostheses. For HCDS, prostheses were needed to replace primarily knees and hips and, to a lesser degree, shoulders and ankles.

According to Fortune Business Insights, the global orthopedic implant market size was $37.1 billion in 2023 and has a revenue forecast of $56.1 billion for 2030. Those who worked in orthopedic implant sales were *all men*—men who had to convince other men (that is, orthopedic surgeons) to use their ever-increasingly expensive products. If I wanted to break from this, I had to break from the entire culture.

Be Ready for a Fistfight

The implant industry was definitely in the business of selling the most expensive products to their best customers—joint replacements were sold to big general hospitals that in turn supplied them à la carte to the surgeons. This was a serious conundrum for HCDS, one that we continued to struggle with. Our goal was to provide knee and hip replacements that were lower in cost and higher in quality. We had been creative enough to achieve some of the lowest infection rates in the country, as well as develop an HCDS team who was working with world-class efficiency. It was the implant cost that was a problem—and, by the way, remains so to this day.

As an orthopedic surgeon as well as the founder of a healthcare delivery system, I was fortunate to have had a diverse career as I routinely moved from one field to another. As a result, I did not have enough time to develop deep networks in the implant world. In order to do so, I would have had to incur entertainment and travel expenses, as well as lavish consulting contracts. All of which I avoided during my entire career.

If I had been encumbered by the lavish gifts of the implant industry, I believe I would have lost the creativity needed for innovation in total joint delivery. I needed implants that were cheaper but still high quality, something Medicare soon began to realize. HCDS remained an outsider to this implant network, and as a result we forced our competitors to produce some competitive pricing. A modest win, but it didn't come easily.

One discipline that taught me a lot during my years in sports medicine was wrestling. Wrestlers work harder to prepare for their matches than any other professional athletes with whom I have ever worked. They train religiously. Because each wrestler knows that on match day it will be just them alone in the arena against the opponent. Everyone in the stands will be looking at them. There will be no one else there to fight their battle. And most wrestlers will tell you their coaches advise them to leave it all on the mat. They are supposed to come off that mat having exhausted every limb, every muscle, every strategy—leaving nothing behind and nothing to chance. The best wrestlers prepare and then on the day of their match, execute. They fight their battle and do so with one goal: to become victorious.

When you are starting any venture, it's imperative to have a wrestler's mental toughness and grit. It's the only way to get through the tough times.

Summary: A Few Last Words

I've often been asked the following question: "Since you had to start a healthcare delivery system from scratch, weren't you worried that you might not be able to catch up to the others?" My answer was that if HCDS was innovating constantly, we wouldn't be competing with general healthcare providers and hospitals. We also wouldn't be competing with companies like us (because at the time there was no one like us—or at least very few of them). So it wasn't a matter of catching up. It was a matter of being in another lane. I was running my own race.

My wife used to run track, in particular the 400. She had to run one full lap around the track. Her lane assignment depended on her qualifying time. The prime spot was to be right in the middle. If you've ever watched the Olympics, you know that the runners line up at what appears to be an angle. The person running in the middle lane can see half the field in front of them, and the rest of the runners behind them won't catch up until three-quarters of the way through the race. The key, however, is not to worry about the other runners. A cardinal rule is to never look over your shoulder. Each runner runs straight ahead at their own pace and knows when to break out. It never helps to see the full field. In fact, those far behind have the worst position because they see everyone ahead of them. They may try to match their pace to speed up too quickly and end up running out of steam by the end. They could become overwhelmed by how much they have to make up and might mentally quit before they even get started. In contrast, those in the front, who can't see behind them, may think they can coast in, never really worrying about the competition, and then be overtaken in the last few strides. It's as much a mental race as a physical one. In the 400m, there are also multiple curves. You're not running straight, and you need to constantly adjust your strategy. All parts of the race are not equal. Your only goal should be to focus on your own race—your own stride, pacing, and strategy. That's what gets you over the finish line.

Running HCDS was like running the 400. I had to stay in my lane and avoid pacing myself based on the runners in front of me or behind me. The reality was, I wasn't lucky enough to be in the middle lane. I was on the outside, and I set my own stride and ran my own race. Even if my well-established competitors had all the advantages, even if they were in the middle lane, it didn't guarantee a win for them.

I've always believed that in order to have a fighting chance in the race, you have to possess a certain level of excitement. The word "passion" is overused, but it was absolutely critical that I had passion for what I was doing and that I loved what I did. This was true even when the money was not there, as hard as that was to swallow. People need money to survive—for their mortgages, education, and healthcare. Yes, there was a time when I had a mortgage, school loans, and a family to provide for—I know what it means to need money. But the minute money supersedes passion, it never works. On the other hand, if there is enough passion and it's sustained for the right amount of time, there's always money that comes along with it.

It wasn't always easy, but we persisted by maximizing creativity.

One way we did this was by treating other physicians respectfully. Instead of alienating our colleagues, we worked to make them part of our new network. Most of the orthopedic physicians in the area joined our network.

Another lesson Clay Christensen taught me was that in order to sustain innovation, established companies often needed to create independent divisions or even spin off entities to break away from their network. We followed his advice when developing a healthcare management company and a healthcare real estate and asset management company.

The most important lesson Clay taught me was that when you're striving to be innovative—striving to have these creative ideas that knock it out of the park and change people's lives—you have to form the right group of people who are going to do it with you. You have to separate them by their zones of genius, then give them each their own identity and space to innovate, and then bring them together.

Another insight I learned from the process of innovation and creating something out of nothing is that—as with the universe itself—all things that are created continue to expand and grow. If it's not growing, it's dying. The more you create, the more you grow. One idea leads to another.

When you get to the implementation stage, you will find yourself moving back into preparation, incubation, insight, and evaluation over and over again, as more creations are born out of your ideas.

I left HCDS in 2019 after thirty years. It is still running today and is now integrated into a large regional hospital network. As you can tell, creating HCDS didn't happen overnight. Progressing from preparation to implementation takes time—but in the process, I not only created something bigger than myself that helped others, but also learned invaluable skills and learned to apply them with tools I acquired. Plus, I went on journeys I never expected or imagined when I started my career as a surgeon. And certainly, I came a long way from being an immigrant's son living in New York, drawing with pencils for fun. All told, from the start to the end of my journey, I became more of who I was always meant to be. Not only did I create HCDS, but I also created a new version of myself (several, in fact: systems engineer, surgeon, entrepreneur, community member, political activist, real estate owner, sculptor, artist) and, more importantly, I became a person with more insights, clarity, passion, joy, and love than when I started this incredible journey of becoming more creative, more fully human.

Jump-Start Your Creativity

Writing prompts for your journal:

- Do you have the passion to keep going? What keeps you up at night? What keeps you motivated?
- Who can help you fulfill your creative vision? What experts can you surround yourself with?
- What areas can you develop more?
- In the process of building or elaborating, have you realized that you need to build something else? Do you know where to begin? Who to ask? Do you need to go back to the preparation stage?
- Reflect on your creative journey. What have you learned about yourself? What skills and tools do you have now that you didn't have before you started?

PART 3

Beyond the Studio

CHAPTER 9

Creativity in Everyday Life

I said in the beginning that the creative process is not linear. You will be incubating while implementing new ideas. You'll be evaluating one set of ideas while preparing for another creative endeavor. You may be forming insights while you're evaluating and implementing two different creative solutions. One problem begets another, and you will have infinite opportunities to put the creative process to good use throughout your life.

I hope that by now we have established that creativity isn't confined to artists' studios or the realm of painters, writers, and sculptors. It's a fundamental approach—a way of life—that can be applied wherever problems arise, decisions need to be made, or new ideas are needed. Whether you are in your office, your warehouse, your car, personal relationships, community group, or even your kitchen, the stages of creativity—preparation, incubation, insight, evaluation, and implementation—are universally applicable.

The Power of Routine and Preparation

As someone who has transitioned from engineering to art school to medical school to the OR to the entrepreneurial world to sculpting to my most recent endeavors in writing and regenerative organic farming, I can attest that routines and preparation form the backbone of consistent creativity. As a surgeon I had several routines that kept me grounded, from washing up to meticulously laying out my surgical instruments and tools and establishing a systematic workflow. These routines ensured efficiency and minimized surprises, creating an environment conducive to innovative thinking. Even though I am no longer in the OR, I apply that same discipline across all areas: organizing my workspace, planning my day, even preparing my morning breakfast the night before. I make sure I am at my writing desk by 4:00 AM. And after an hour and half of writing, I have my breakfast. This is followed by a garden walk, and then I meet with my staff in the sculpture studio. I take my lunch at the same time every day and follow it with a short, restorative nap. I have a short stint at my writing desk and then I head back to the sculpture studio. I like to wrap up my day in the gym and then shower before dinner. Lights are out by 9:00 PM. Rinse. Repeat.

Routines make it possible for me to be creative. If I don't have to think about what I am going to eat, wear, or do at a certain time, I leave creative space open in my mind. I realize I am in a very fortunate position at this point in my life. But it wasn't always the case; I was sculpting when I was a surgeon. I found time before and after work to draw, sketch, and sculpt. The key is to find a schedule and routine that work for you. I know single moms who get up at 4:30 AM, before their children wake up, so they can have that time to themselves—to write, draw, paint, and work out. Some people aren't morning people. They prefer the nights. That's fine! No judgment. Find a time that works for you, and then by all means work with the time you have. You can do anything in as little as an hour or two a day. Over time those hours add up. If you're writing a book for an hour a day, usually that means one to two pages per day—over the course of a year, that can add up to a book! The same goes for any creative pursuit. Starting a business? Inventing something? Break it down into small, doable chunks, and then create a sustainable routine that you can work with consistently.

Set up and prepare yourself for the routine. People who jog first thing in the morning put out their running shorts, T-shirt, and sneakers the night before so they don't have to think about it in the morning. They can just get up, get dressed, and go. Set yourself up for similar success. Lay out your work the night before.[1]

Like laying out ingredients for a recipe or the tools before you work, these routines set the stage for clarity, focus, and productivity.

Incubation and Insight in Daily Life

Incubation and insight are stages we all need to embrace in our everyday lives. As I get older, I am more aware of the time I have, and therefore I pay more attention to how and with whom I spend it. I enjoy spending time with my wife, walking through the woods on our farm in the Poconos, walking our dogs, visiting with neighbors, and eating country dinners. But I also enjoy getting into the city to take in a Broadway show or visit galleries or museums. One never knows where inspiration might strike. You have to actively pursue it. Get out into

---

1. I find it helpful to study the routines of writers and visual artists. I highly recommend Mason Currey's *Daily Rituals: How Artists Work* (Knopf, 2013) and *Daily Rituals: Women at Work* (Knopf, 2019).

the world. Take day trips and discover new vistas and landscapes. Taste new foods. Talk to people who are different from you. Listen to them. Ask questions. Instead of trying to get them to think like you do, try to understand why they think the way they do.

Then step away again. As you know by now, insight arrives when our subconscious processes align and we get those moments of clarity or "aha" experiences. Whether you're working on a team project, parenting, or navigating a complex relationship, giving yourself room for thought and reflection unlocks solutions that immediate effort might obscure.

Evaluation and Implementation Are All Around You

The beauty of understanding the stages of the creative process is that once you know them and start using them in your daily life, you'll find they are applicable to almost every area. The skills you use in the evaluation stage can be used in personal relationships. Having a tense conversation with a partner or a child? The evaluation stage will help you ask thoughtful questions and listen deeply. You'll be much more likely to take a few minutes to take in all the information before jumping to judgments and conclusions. Try to walk in other people's shoes. Get into their minds. Sit with their feelings—not yours. Theirs. It's not easy, but it's how you learn about others, and eventually yourself. Amazing insights form if you have the courage—and humility—to set your ego aside and just listen to what another has to say. And to refrain from judgment or being defensive. Simply listen.

At work? Stop what you're doing and go back to the evaluation JTBD, connect and combine ideas, choose the best ones, weigh the options, and test the assumptions.

Then it's time to take action. Life is iterative. You're never, ever going to get it right on the first go-around. Trust me! Life is about failing fast and failing forward! You mess up, you learn where you went wrong, and you go back and fix what needs to be fixed and try again. This goes for relationships too. No one is perfect, and we would all be a lot better off if we remembered that and gave others the grace and forgiveness we expect for ourselves. The better we get at revising on the go, the better we get at living.

The undercurrent of all life's efforts is rooted in your creative process. But your routine, your actions, and your ability to connect and empathize with others will keep that creative undercurrent flowing. Your creative process is the engine that allows you to grow, flourish, and ultimately become fully human.

CONCLUSION: FULLY HUMAN

> So God created mankind in his own image, in the image of God he created them.
>
> —Genesis 2:17

Michelangelo's most notable work is a ceiling painting—none other than the massive ceiling in the Sistine Chapel. In this vast and breathtaking scene, Michelangelo and his team illustrated the biblical creation narrative from the book of Genesis. The first book of the Bible, Genesis, recounts the poetic parable of God's creation of the universe. One of the most popular scenes within the mural, one that has been re-created all over the world, is the Creation of Adam. In this section, God, who looks like Michelangelo himself, leans over and nearly touches the finger of Adam with his own.

Whenever I see this fresco, I think of this line in Genesis: "So God created mankind in his own image, in the image of God he created them." I also chuckle to myself, thinking of the laugh Michelangelo must have had when he painted himself into this iconic scene. He is, indeed, God—the creator—of the painting. And he was right to paint himself as the creator. After all, God, the creator, made humans in his image. Thus, all humans are creators. That is our purpose here on earth. It was written down for us thousands of years ago in ancient texts, and it is visible in all areas of our lives.[1] In fact, when I think of being alive, being human, I think of being creative. To live, one must create. Not creating, then, is to die. I have seen many people die long before they were buried because they have ceased to create.

In this book, I have argued that all of us are creatives—whether small "c" (living our daily lives creatively) or big "C" (transforming and changing all of humanity's lives in the process). When we are creating, we are expanding and growing. Our intellect grows as we study, investigate, and gather knowledge to solve the problems we face. We are constantly preparing, incubating, connecting, evaluating, and elaborating on ideas. We are creators; the five stages of preparation, incubation, insight, evaluation, and implementation are always at work.

Our relationships flourish when we create, and when we are creating, I would argue that we are the truest, most authentic versions of ourselves. And when we become these authentic versions of ourselves, we automatically attract other like-minded individuals—those who also want to create, problem solve, grow, learn, play, and maybe even

---

1. The concept of humans created in God's image (Imago Dei) originates in the Hebrew Bible (Genesis 1:26–27), which is foundational for Judaism and Christianity. The Koran also affirms God as the Creator: "Allah is the Creator of all things, and He is, over all things, Disposer of affairs." (Surah Az-Zumar 39:62. "He created you and formed you and made your forms beautiful." (Surah Ghafir 40:64). The Sikh Guru Granth Sahib describes God as the Creator and humans as divine reflections: "He Himself created Himself; He Himself assumed His Name." (Ang 463) The Hindu Upanishads and Bhagavad Gita present Brahman (the ultimate reality) as the source of all creation.

change the world. Humanity is, after all, the center of creativity. As humans, we create for ourselves and each other. Art, music, theater, dancing, culture, and food are all born from the creative spirit, and all are meeting points of humanity. Attend any concert, live theatrical event, or movie and watch as humans of all walks of life, socioeconomic statuses, races, and religions come together in shared admiration. Such settings are magical. But so are offices, shopping centers, hospitals, banks, schools, factories, and construction zones. Walk through any office setting or workplace and you will witness people coming together to solve problems, innovate, and, yes, create.

Creativity makes us more apt to be unified and harmonious. Being creative serves as a kind of centrifuge—a separator of all that is good and life-giving from that which destroys or harms. For the root of the word "creativity" is "create"—to give life to something. This is the exact opposite of killing or harming. Therefore, morality is imperative in being a creative. You must have a strong sense of what is right and wrong or just and unjust to be creative. True creativity benefits others; it doesn't harm others. That is not to say that it doesn't make people feel uncomfortable. The greatest works of art are usually acts of rebellion. They hold a mirror up to the world and show it what it could be. As the Mexican poet Cesar A. Cruz once said, "Art should comfort the disturbed, and disturb the comfortable." Doing so leads us to a spiritual awakening, an understanding of who we are and why we are here. Ultimately, creating shows us there is a power greater than ourselves working through us every step of the way. Creativity requires a level of surrender to ideas, thoughts, and inspiration from beyond yourself. And once you've reached this point, you are in some ways not just fully human but fully divine as well. For being a creative is the point at which, as when God reaches toward Adam, human and God become one.

My ultimate hope is that after reading this book you feel inspired to create—not just in your profession, or your interests, but in your daily life. After all, you were created to do just that. I hope you see that there is potential to create in everything and that *you are creative.*

And remember the words "In the beginning, God created . . ." The key words here are "beginning," "God," and "created."

You know what to do now. You have the stages, the processes, the behaviors, the divine artist within you. All you have to do is . . .

Begin.

APPENDIX

Notes on Names, Terms, and Further Thoughts Not Included in the Chapters

Introduction

Great Resignation

Also known as the "Big Quit." Beginning in early 2021, many American employees resigned from their jobs. This occurred during the COVID-19 pandemic. The main reason was job dissatisfaction. Today's workforce is younger and more diverse and includes more women. These people are turning away from the rags-to-riches success story and searching for success on their own terms. While generating wealth remains important, self-expression and personal fulfillment are also stressed.

Graham Wallas (1858–1932)

British psychologist and founder of the London School of Economics. Wallas has been formative in my creative research. He wrote *The Art of Thought*, which outlined four stages of creativity: preparation, incubation, illumination, and verification. Especially helpful was chapter 4, "Stages of Control in the Art of Thought."

Mihaly Csikszentmihalyi (1934–2021)

Hungarian American psychologist known for his research in creativity as well as for being the "father of flow"—a mental state of optimal performance. Csikszentmihalyi has been foundational in my creativity research. As founder of the field of positive psychology, he devoted much of his career to trying to figure out how one lives a happy life, which for me means being fully human, at the center of which is creativity.

Keith Sawyer

Professor of educational innovation at the University of North Carolina. Sawyer is an expert in creativity and innovation and completed his PhD under Mihaly Csikszentmihalyi. He has been foundational in my creativity research. His book *Zig Zag* is less academic than Csikszentmihalyi's work and more helpful for understanding the creative process.

Jobs to Be Done

I borrowed this term from Clay Christensen, who coined it in 2005. The main concept is that customers don't buy products. They pull products into their lives because they are trying to make progress. The progress they're trying to make is the Jobs to Be Done (JTBD). This concept is especially important in healthcare delivery, where the main customer is the patient and the complexity they need to navigate is the healthcare system.

Chapter 1

Marino Marini (1901–1980)

Italian sculptor and painter whose work was influenced by Etruscan art. Marini has been one of a handful of Italians who have influenced my art. Over the years, I have worked to refine the image of the female nude. Marini has taught me how to be as sensitive to form and surface as the Etruscans of the south were. He also taught me to strive for the inner tension of the straining figure that we found in the north (Marini saw this in Switzerland and Germany, and I saw this in Belgium and Holland).

Arturo Martini (1889–1947)

Important Italian sculptor between World War I and World War II. Martini was a teacher of Marino Marini and was a professor at the Scuola d'Arte di Villa Reale near Milan until succeeded by Marini. My study of Martini and his ability to definitively move from figurative classism to modernism has helped in my sculpture and painting.

Etruscans

Ancient people of Italy who lived between the Tiber and the Arno Rivers. The Etruscan civilization reached its height in the sixth century BC. It was an artistic culture that produced distinctive terra-cotta and bronze sculpture. A place that I never tire of is the National Etruscan Museum of Villa Giulia. I highly recommend visiting if you're ever afforded the opportunity.

Renaissance—Italian and Northern

Northern (Belgium, Germany, and Holland) Renaissance art is better known for its realism and detail. Italian Renaissance art was more colorful and idealized the human form. Together they shaped Western art's development. Even though my family is from southern Europe, my studies in northern Europe taught me how advanced the north was even before the Renaissance started in Italy.

Benito Mussolini (1883–1945)

Dictator and principal founder of fascism. This man and his politics were the principal reasons my mother's father moved his family and business to New York.

STEM

Abbreviation often used to represent four closely connected areas: science, technology, engineering, and math. This term wasn't used until much later, but in the late 1960s, when I was an undergraduate engineering major, America was in a space and arms race with Russia. Graduates with science, technology, engineering, or math degrees were highly sought after not only by companies in the military-industrial world but also by the finance world of Wall Street.

Abstract expressionism

A form of abstract art developed by American painters in the 1940s–1960s. It is nonrepresentational and without a single focal point. The abstract expressionism movement, which began in New York, shifted the world's art focus from Paris to New York. As such, it is sometimes known as the New York school.

Jackson Pollock (1912–1956)

American abstract expressionist painter known especially for his large paintings made from 1947 to 1951. Pollock, together with Willem de Kooning and Mark Rothko, was at the center of the New York school.

Frank Stella (1936–2024)

American painter and sculptor who is best known as a minimalist artist—that is, an artist who does not make paintings or sculptures about the things we see in the world. Minimalist art, pop art, and conceptual art were all in their developmental stages in the late 1960s while I was studying in New York.

Donald Judd (1928–1994)

American painter and sculptor who was associated with minimalism. Judd was a landmark figure in the history of postwar art. Of interest to me is the fact that he was a writer as well as a visual artist. He wrote about the importance of art, land preservation, and gaining knowledge from experience.

Pop art movement

An art movement that was very popular in the late 1960s. Pop art is based on simple, bold images of everyday objects—for example, Andy Warhol's soup cans. I remember Warhol being the talk of New York and recall seeing him and his entourage in Washington Square Park.

Conceptual art movement

An art movement that surfaced in the 1960s. In conceptual art, the idea (concept) is more important than the actual artwork. What it looks like doesn't matter as long as the idea comes across. As a visual artist, I have often struggled with this approach, but I remain respectful of it, nonetheless.

Parris Island

In 1915, Parris Island in South Carolina became the main Marine Corps training center, and it remains so to this day. A number of people I knew went through Parris Island on their way to Vietnam. Some returned in coffins. This was a terrible time.

Grumman Aerospace, Bethpage, New York

A major producer of military and civilian aircraft during much of the twentieth century. Grumman was the production site for the Apollo Lunar Module and the F-14 Tomcat. In 1994, it merged with the Northrop Corporation to form Northrop Grumman. Although I spent only three years at Grumman, I owe the company a debt of gratitude. These were formative years for someone just finishing engineering school. The Grumman family not only introduced me to the real world but allowed me to support myself and study economics. Finally, I was privileged to be part of a company that made history.

Neil Armstrong (1930–2012)

American astronaut who in 1969, at the age of thirty-eight, was the first man to walk on the moon. I remember Neil Armstrong visiting Grumman after his moon walk. He was asked what it felt like to be the first human to view the earth from the moon. His answer was that he never realized how beautiful our home planet was and that we should do everything to preserve it.

Bernard Schmitz (b. 1915)

German-born economist who immigrated to the United States after World War II. Schmitz was a full-time consultant at Grumman Aerospace when I met him in 1969. This quiet but intense man, who was in his fifties when I worked with him, taught me how to appreciate and enjoy finance and economics.

Peter Paul Rubens (1577–1640)

German-born painter who lived in Antwerp, Belgium, from the age of ten. His house with a studio in the center of Antwerp was an Italian palazzo, a small city palace. The Rubens house and its gardens were a source of inspiration for me during the years I lived and studied in Antwerp.

Julien "Jan" Fautrez (1914–1996)

Chair of human anatomy at Ghent University. Fautrez authored 150 articles in international journals as well as three books. He taught me how to love, understand, draw, and teach the anatomy of the musculoskeletal system.

Twyla Tharp (b. 1941)

American choreographer whose work traverses the boundary between modern dance and ballet. I especially enjoyed her book *The Creativity Habit* and appreciated her rituals for preparations or routines to get into a creative state. And I loved how she showed up for work every day and accepted the ebbs and flows of creativity.

Cicero (106–43 BC)
Roman poet and philosopher as well as a great orator and shrewd politician. Cicero is famous for many quotes, but one of my favorites is "Any man can make mistakes, but only an idiot persists in his error." I never had time to formally study the classics, but there are a few authors, such as Cicero, who have taught me a thing or two.

Chapter 2

Masaki Watanabe (1911–1995)
Japanese orthopedic surgeon who is considered the original pioneer of present-day arthroscopic surgery. This "father of arthroscopy" opened an entirely new field of orthopedic surgery for my generation. I was told by those who knew Dr. Watanabe that he rarely spoke of his own achievement—he did not have to. His peers, a number of whom were my teachers, did the talking for him.

Robert W. Jackson (1932–2010)
Canadian orthopedic surgeon who is widely credited for bringing arthroscopic surgery to North America. He was a full professor in the Department of Surgery at the University of Toronto. I met Dr. Jackson when he was a visiting professor in Boston. I remember him telling me how he taught Dr. Watanabe English in exchange for Watanabe teaching him knee arthroscopy.

Robert E. Leach (b. 1932)
Orthopedic surgeon in Boston, Massachusetts. Dr. Leach was the chair of the Department of Orthopedic Surgery at Boston University. He was also the head physician of the US Olympics and editor emeritus

of the *American Journal of Sports Medicine.* Dr. Leach was one of the most influential people in my life. Having himself started from humble beginnings as the immigrant son of a coal miner, he was a role model who showed me how to use arthroscopic surgery to help others.

Mario Andretti (b. 1940)
Italian-born American racing driver. Mario personifies the American Dream—he is an immigrant who achieved fame and fortune. Few suit stardom as much as this man of unforced charm and natural talent. It has always been a privilege for me to have him as a patient and a friend.

Lehigh Valley
A region that sits in the economic center of the United States on the border of Pennsylvania and New Jersey. It is a short drive from the Lehigh Valley to either New York City or Philadelphia. The people of the Lehigh Valley trusted me, a young surgeon, and gave me the privilege to treat their families, build a practice, and eventually create an innovative healthcare hospital network.

John Havlicek (1940–2019)
An American professional basketball player who spent his entire career with the Boston Celtics (1962–1978). During his career, he won eight NBA championships. Throughout his career with the Celtics, Havlicek remained both a patient and a close friend of my mentor, Dr. Robert Leach.

Chapter 3

Malcolm Gladwell (b. 1963)
English-born Canadian author and journalist. His book *Outliers* challenges the idea that success is based only on individual talent and discusses how to create a culture of success. Gladwell claims that repetition

is key and came up with the requirement of 10,000 reps. Gladwell is not an academic; he is a journalist. He is not formally trained in any of the sciences and is the first to say so. He is basically a storyteller and a good one.

Anders Ericsson (1947–2020)

Swedish psychologist and professor of psychology at Florida State University. He was an expert in the psychological nature of expertise and human performance—focusing on extended deliberate practice beyond one's comfort zone (in 1993). It is this work that was cited in Malcolm Gladwell's *Outliers* (2008) and done so incorrectly. Ericsson felt that deliberate (improved) practice was key.

Aldo Rossi (1931–1997)

Though I don't write about him in this book or chapter 3, I was inspired by this Italian architect and designer, the first Italian to receive the Pritzker Architecture Prize. Like many sculptors, I have a special respect for architects. The great ones like Carlo Scarpa (another Italian) as well as Americans such as Louis Kahn and Frank Lloyd Wright were visual artists as well as architects.

Il Teatro del Mondo

I also didn't cover this in chapter 3, but when I think of inspiring pieces of architecture I think of the floating building designed for the Venice Biennale in 1980 by Aldo Rossi. Il Teatro del Mondo recalled the Venetian tradition of the wooden floating theater.

Chapter 4

Clay Christensen (1952–2020)

American management consultant, author, and professor at Harvard Business School. Christensen coined the term "disruptive innovation."

This is a process by which a product or service takes root initially in simple applications, at the bottom of the market, and then keeps moving up the market until it displaces an established competitor. Christensen's lectures, books, and meetings always left me with a better understanding of the complex healthcare delivery world. Plus, he was an incredible human being. I miss him.

Peter Drucker (1909–2005)

Austrian-born management consultant and educator. Drucker is considered the father of modern management—he famously said, "Culture eats strategy for breakfast." He spent twenty-two years at New York University as a professor of management. I can still remember him standing up at a meeting and telling us in his German drawl not to try and invent the future but rather to look out the window because the future was already happening. I used this advice throughout my career.

Systems thinking / Jay Forrester (1918–2016)

Jay Forrester is the father of systems thinking. He created this method of problem-solving in 1956 while at the Sloan School of Management at MIT. Systems thinking is the ability to perform problem-solving in a complex system. It is a holistic approach to the factors and their interactions that contributes to a possible outcome. Example: A car is a system. It is a product of the interaction of its parts, not just the sum of its parts. If you take the car apart, it is no longer a car since it has lost its essential functions. Other examples include the human body and a healthcare hospital network. In designing a healthcare delivery network, systems thinking was foundational.

Design thinking / Herbert Simon (1916–2001)

Nobel laureate Herbert Simon is the father of design thinking. He first mentioned design as a method of problem-solving in his 1969 book, *The Science of the Artificial.* Design thinking follows a user-based approach to devise innovative solutions for complex problems. Rapid prototyping and testing through observation form the core of many design processes.

Michael Porter (b. 1947)

Professor of business at Harvard Business School. Porter is a leading authority on strategy and competitiveness. I am particularly grateful that Professor Porter allowed my team to present our healthcare delivery business model in 2018 at the Harvard Business School.

Sir John Charnley (1911–1982)

English orthopedic surgeon who pioneered the hip replacement that relieved pain in hundreds of thousands of people. This hip was composed of a plastic socket and metal ball, which were cemented into place. I never met Professor Charnley, but I was taught hip surgery by one of his students when I trained in Boston. I would hear stories of his remarkable surgical skills and his ability to complete a hip operation three times faster than his peers.

Anthony DePalma (1904–2005)

Orthopedic surgeon and professor at Thomas Jefferson University; the son of immigrant Italian parents from Alberona (population: 980) in southeast Italy. Dr. DePalma wrote several orthopedic textbooks that are considered standards. He was a visiting professor while I was training in Boston. A master surgeon, he knew where to put his incision, was kind to soft tissues, and worked quickly, resulting in minimal blood loss.

Georgia O'Keeffe (1887–1986)

American painter best known for her paintings of flowers and desert landscapes. She was the first female artist to exhibit at MoMA. I admire O'Keeffe the painter as well as the photographer. She said, "To create one's world in any of the arts takes courage."

Warren Buffett (b. 1930)
Longtime chairman of Berkshire Hathaway. Buffett focuses on long-term value, identifying companies that he considers undervalued by the market. It has always amused me that he still lives in the same five-bedroom house that he bought in 1956 for $30,000.

George de Mestral (1907–1990)
Swiss electrical engineer who invented the hook and loop fastener, which he called Velcro. De Mestral got the idea in his thirties, but it took more than twenty years to produce the innovation. Of additional interest to me is that he worked odd jobs to pay for engineering school. I like this guy.

Jean-Claude Killy (b. 1943)
French World Cup alpine ski racer. Killy dominated the sport in the late 1960s and finished with three gold medals in the 1968 Winter Olympics. My mentor, Dr. Leach, who was an avid skier and the head physician of the US Olympic Ski Team, would often discuss Killy's injury and return to sport.

Sistine Chapel
A chapel in the pope's residence in Vatican City. The Sistine Chapel was built from 1473–1481 and is famous for its Renaissance ceiling paintings created by Michelangelo from 1508–1512. Actually, Michelangelo considered himself a sculptor and not a painter and was vocal about it. He was forced to paint the Sistine Chapel by Pope Julius II.

Isaac Newton (1643–1727)
British scientist who discovered the laws of gravity. Newton also developed laws of motion and invented calculus (with Gottfried Wilhelm Leibniz).

Archimedes (287 BC–c. 211 BC)

The most famous mathematician and inventor in ancient Greece. Archimedes's principle is useful for calculating the volume of an object that does not have a regular shape. The object can be submerged and the volume of the fluid displaced is equal to the volume of the object. Archimedes's principle can also be used to calculate density or specific gravity.

3M Company / Spencer Silver (1941–2021) / Art Fry (b. 1931)

Silver and Fry both worked for the 3M Company and are the co-inventors of Post-it Notes. Silver created the adhesive, but Fry was responsible for taking it to market and creating a business. I am a big fan of Post-it Notes. They are everywhere in my study rooms. All sorts of colors and all sorts of sizes, lined and unlined.

Healthcare Delivery System (HCDS)

The healthcare company I founded, but the name has been changed for legal purposes.

Medici dynasty

A powerful, art-loving Italian banking family who dominated Florence from the fifteenth to the eighteenth centuries. Through their patronage of major artists like Michelangelo, the Medici produced the framework for the Renaissance. In fact, as a teenager, Michelangelo lived with the Medici family for four years before going on to create his *David* and *Pietà*.

Charles Darwin (1809–1882) / John Gould (1804–1881)

Gould helped identify species in the collection of 450 birds that Darwin presented to the Zoological Society in 1837. This identification showed that the birds were not different varieties of the same species but rather a number of distinct species, each from its own isolated island. This was the beginning of the innovative theory of evolution.

Capitation

A way of reimbursing healthcare providers in which they receive a set amount of money to cover services that are supposedly predictable. The provider organization assumes the risk for the set amount. If the cost of care is more than the capitation payment, the provider absorbs the loss. Risk-assuming providers face increasing exposure to operating losses and may be forced to reduce patient benefits. This threatens the patient-provider relationship.

General hospital business model—"everything to everybody"

The principle of trying to provide any healthcare good and service to whoever walks through the door, whatever their diagnosis may be. The general hospital has to provide a product that is not well-defined, for which the result is uncertain, and for which payments are made by government and private insurers. Finally, the industry is dominated by nonprofit providers, which shields them from paying taxes. (See *The Innovator's Prescription* by Clayton Christensen or "Disrupting the Hospital Business Model," *Forbes*, March 30, 2009.)

Bethlehem Steel

An American steelmaking company headquartered in Bethlehem, Pennsylvania. From its founding in 1857 to its closure in 2003, Bethlehem Steel was one of the world's largest steel-producing companies and a symbol of American manufacturing leadership across the world. Bethlehem steel was used to construct NYC's George Washington and Verrazzano Bridges, the Empire State and Chrysler Buildings, and Rockefeller Center. Among other notable projects, the Golden Gate Bridge and the Hoover Dam were also produced with Bethlehem Steel.

In November 1995, the iconic blast furnaces in the Bethlehem Steel South Side plant closed down. At the time Bethlehem Steel closed, HCDS was a major healthcare subcontractor. I had the privilege of treating both management and union leadership.

Vertically integrated healthcare network

A network formed by organizing doctors, hospitals, and other providers into groups in order to increase the quality, decrease the cost, and increase patient access. At HCDS we were able to optimally integrate the entire process, from preadmission testing to the surgery process to rehabilitation, a significant decrease in complication and infection rates.

Millennials / Gen Z

Millennial members were born between 1981 and 1996. Gen Z members were born between 1997 and 2012. Millennials' customer service expectations tend to be greater than those of Gen Z. Indeed, as we found at HCDS, both Millennials and Gen Z were looking to us for self-service educational materials. If they can fix it themselves, they will. Millennials, especially, wanted speedy replies and timely customer service.

Chapter 5

Battle of Munda

The final battle in Julius Caesar's civil war. The Battle of Munda occurred in 45 BC in present-day southern Spain. After winning this battle, Caesar returned to Rome and was elected dictator. It seems that Julius Caesar was quite good at "incubation." In 47 BC, while civil war was still going on in Rome, Caesar took Cleopatra on a monthslong cruise on the Nile.

Claude Monet (1840–1926)

French painter who was one of the founders of impressionism. Monet is well known for the 250 water lily paintings that he made over a thirty-year period.

Citicorp / John Reed (b. 1939)

Reed was named CEO of Citicorp in 1984. He is credited with advancing the adoption of the ATM across the United States. In 2004, he was named chairman of the New York Stock Exchange. One of the most famous memos in banking history was thirty-seven-year-old Reed's "Memo from the Beach" (1976), which described the vision and thinking for a consumer banking business that even today would be forward-thinking.

Combinatory play

A term used by Albert Einstein for the process of coming up with unrelated ideas and combining them in a way that produces something that is new. This mental process of linking or associating one idea with an often-unrelated idea has also been called associative thinking. It has been around a long time—Aristotle believed that this type of mental process was basic to human thinking. Today, both psychologists and neuroscientists continue to study this process.

Winston Churchill (1874–1965)

British prime minister (1940–1945) during most of World War II. Churchill was also an accomplished writer and painter. In addition, he enjoyed manual labor on his estate, Chartwell. He was an avid bricklayer, always ready to help fix a slate roof and build ponds for his koi fish. It appears he knew the importance of incubation in the creative process.

Milton Glaser (1929–2020)
American graphic designer. Glaser designed the "I ♥ New York" logo on scrap paper with red crayon while sitting in a taxi in New York traffic. Like many creative people, he thought working with your hands is good for your brain. He also felt ideas should be properly tested using pen, brush, and then a computer. Glaser always stressed the value of initially searching for ideas through drawing in order to produce creative designs.

Default mode network (DMN)
An area of the brain that is active when a person is awake but not focusing on anything in particular, for example daydreaming or letting their mind wander. The DMN, when combined with other brain networks, is important for creativity. So we can say that when a person is not in the middle of a mentally demanding task, the brain shifts into "default." Here's an example: When I am in a new city and following my wife to a restaurant, my mind checks out and my body operates on autopilot. This allows me to daydream. But if I try to get to the same restaurant in the future, I am in trouble!

Cognitive control network (CCN)
Areas of the brain that control memory, attention span, and other functions in response to a task. An example of a thought process that involves the CCN is making a conscious decision to skip dessert after a particularly rich dinner. Another example is staying focused at your workplace instead of checking out Instagram.

Functional magnetic resonance imaging (fMRI)
A type of MRI scan that measures small changes in the blood flow in the brain based on brain activity. Tracking these blood flow changes and comparing them to what a person is doing at the time of the test

allows the technician to "map" brain activity. Brain cells, called neurons, have higher oxygen levels when they are active. The fMRI monitors these blood oxygen levels in real time to detect brain activity.

Alexander Liberman (1912–1999)

Editorial director of Condé Nast for over fifty years. Liberman defined contemporary magazine culture. But his impact was also felt in the art world: he was an author, photographer, painter, and sculptor. Liberman was known for his large, red steel sculptures and geometric paintings. He was in every sense of the phrase a multifunctional creative.

Lin-Manuel Miranda (b. 1980)

American composer, writer, and actor. Miranda has created stage productions such as *Hamilton*, which combines different types of music: pop, hip-hop, soul, and traditional show tunes. He wrote *Hamilton* over seven years and then played Alexander Hamilton on Broadway. *Hamilton*, which opened in 2015, is still on Broadway. If you have the opportunity to see it, do so—it's creativity on steroids.

Alexander Hamilton (c. 1757–1804)

Hamilton was one of the United States' founding fathers. He was born in the West Indies. Through his writing skills as a young man, he won a scholarship to study at King's College (now Columbia University) in New York. Hamilton was an officer in the Revolutionary War who became Washington's aide-de-camp. He was a self-taught lawyer who started the Federalist Party—the first US political party. Hamilton later became America's secretary of the treasury. Not only did he die in a duel, but his son did as well.

William Wordsworth (1770–1850)

English poet who was a leader in the Romantic movement, which focused on beauty, emotion, and imagination. Both of Wordsworth's parents died before he was fifteen and he lived with different relatives. Wordsworth developed a love for nature. My favorite Wordsworth quote is "Nature never did betray the heart that loved her."

Insight meditation

Insight meditation is about transforming your level of wisdom. Energy is used to reflect on your thoughts and emotions to gain new understandings and insights. Another type I practice is calming meditation, in which you focus on your breath to produce a peaceful state of mind. Although I use both of these types of meditation, I find neither one easy to do.

Carl Jung (1875–1961)

Swiss psychiatrist who was one of psychology's pioneer figures of the twentieth century. Perhaps the most famous ideas of Jung are his psychological application of spiritual experiences, with a focus on the unconscious and the quest for personal meaning. Jungian archetypes are images that are present in the unconscious of all human beings. In this book, I refer to them as "mental hats."

Political environment related to payment reimbursement

Changes in employment regulations, patient protection, and tax law can affect the levels of payment reimbursement for healthcare providers. For example, a change in tax rates may mean increased government spending for healthcare, while a decreased tax base may mean less government dollars for healthcare. A change in employment law may affect employee overtime and thus staffing needs.

Sorbonne

A university in Paris that was founded eight hundred years ago and remains synonymous with quality and prestige.

Patient encounter

Any type of encounter between a patient and a healthcare provider that involves care and treatment. HCDS often had twelve thousand of these encounters per week on a regular basis.

Chapter 6

J. P. Guilford (1897–1987)

American psychologist who associated divergent thinking with creativity and innovation. Guilford saw divergent thinking as having these key traits:

1. Fluency: producing a large number of ideas
2. Flexibility: producing a variety of approaches to a problem
3. Originality: producing new ideas
4. Elaboration: organizing the details of an idea and carrying it out

My thought is that most human beings have the ability to think in a divergent manner but are not in an environment that fosters it. I believe this is often the case in many business environments where the bottom line is earnings.

IDEO

A design firm founded in Palo Alto, California, in 1993 by David Kelley, who also founded the Stanford Design School to teach and apply design thinking in the academic setting. David Kelley founded IDEO to use the same principles he taught at Stanford in professional settings. IDEO teaches that there are three modes of design thinking: inspiration, ideation, and implementation. The Stanford Design School has five steps to design thinking: empathize, define, ideate, prototype, and test.

Cirque du Soleil

French for "circus of the sun." Cirque du Soleil is a contemporary circus. It is a combination of circus, dance, acrobatics, and music. It stands out for its absence of animals and has a theatrical approach that is based on characters and a story. I have been to a number of these performances. Especially in Las Vegas, they are more a happening than a show!

Alberto Giacometti (1901–1966)

Swiss sculptor and painter. Giacometti worked and lived for most of his adult life in the same small studio in Paris. Although he produced many drawings and paintings, he is most famous for his sculptures—long, elongated figures. He was fascinated with the human head, especially the eyes. In his paintings, he concentrated on the gaze of his sitter. There is no doubt that Giacometti's work can make me feel anxious, but I admire him for the way he handled the art of representation with such persistence. He drew, painted, and sculpted with ferocity—desperate to try and capture what was in front of him.

Cubism

An approach to representing reality in art that was invented by Pablo Picasso and Georges Braque in 1907–1908. Cubism uses geometric shapes to depict humans and other forms, reducing natural forms to the abstract. Cubism allowed for the development of the modern abstract art movement. It was the latter that was able to compete with the newly developed arts of photography and cinema.

Surrealism

The major spokesperson for surrealism was not a visual artist but rather a poet—André Breton. He described surrealism as bringing together conscious and unconscious experiences, thus unlocking creativity. This focus on artistic expression through an explanation of the unconscious mind may work for followers of Sigmund Freud, but it is often lacking for me.

Nikola Tesla (1856–1943)

Serbian American inventor who was a pioneer in modern electricity. Tesla's innovations in energy laid the foundation for electrical delivery as we know it today. Elon Musk's Tesla company name is a tribute to Nikola Tesla—the electrical engineer.

Ron Bass (b. 1942)

American Oscar-winning screenwriter who started writing when he was six years old but stopped because of the criticism he received from his teachers. Bass spent many years practicing law before beginning a screenwriting career at the age of forty. He is a true multidisciplinary creative.

Affordable Care Act (ACA)

Also known as Obamacare. Signed into law in 2010, the ACA was primarily designed to provide low-income individuals with affordable health insurance, thus improving access to healthcare.

Occupational health

An area of healthcare that promotes worksite physical and mental well-being of employees. Occupational health policies improve safety before the first day on the job by making sure new hires can safely perform their jobs. This is done with pre-placement physical exams and pre-employment drug screening. One of the most common occupational health issues is musculoskeletal disorders; others include noise-induced hearing disorders and occupational skin disorders.

Pierre-Auguste Renoir (1841–1919)

French painter who, with his broken brushstrokes, became a leader in the impressionist movement. Renoir developed rheumatoid arthritis when he was around fifty years old. By the age of sixty, he was unable to pick up his paintbrushes (they were strapped to his wrist). He was confined to a wheelchair, but despite his severe disability, he continued to paint. The day he died, at seventy-eight, he had just finished a painting. He turned to his assistant and said, "I think I am starting to understand painting."

Salon

A government art exhibition held each year in Paris in nineteenth-century France. The Salon had a complete monopoly over what new art would be shown. Thus, it also determined the success or failure of painters. The Salon repeatedly rejected a new art movement called impressionism and the painters who were part of it.

Ingresque period

An era of painting done by the impressionist painter Pierre-Auguste Renoir. His painting evolved after an 1881 trip to Italy, during which, after studying such painters as Raphael, he was drawn to classicism. His work became a combination of classical figures and impressionistic landscapes (for example, *Reclining Nude*, 1883). This period was thus called the Ingresque period after the neoclassicist French painter Jean-Auguste-Dominique Ingres.

Associational (associative) thinking

A mental process that associates or combines one idea with another, unrelated idea. Associative thinking is often described as "connecting the dots." By promoting the connection between unrelated ideas, one can arrive at conclusions that might not have been evident. Associative thinking is often divided into two types: divergent thinking and convergent thinking. An example of associative thinking is brainstorming, which consists of generating as many ideas as possible in a constrained amount of time.

Chapter 7

Larry Page (b. 1973) and Sergey Brin (b. 1973)
Cofounders of Google in 1998. Page and Brin met at Stanford University in the 1990s. Both were working on PhDs and collaborating on their research. They transformed a PhD project into a giant technology company. After many years of leading Google, they turned day-to-day operations over to Sundar Pichai.

William Chardack (1915–2006)
A skilled and innovative cardiac surgeon known for his leadership. He and an American engineer, Wilson Greatbatch, worked on a device that developed into a cardiac pacemaker in 1956. Greatbatch, who was working in his backyard barn on an instrument to record the number of heartbeats, accidentally inserted the wrong transistor and was surprised that instead of recording the number of heartbeats, it was imitating the actual number of beats produced by the heart. Greatbatch shared his discovery with Dr. William Chardack. They placed the device in first a dog and then, in 1960, a man. They were able to control the heartbeat.

Plato (c. 428–348 BC) / theory of forms
Plato, a philosopher, and founder of the concept of Platonic Realism. He argued that there are two types of existence: form and matter. The form is the ideal of anything. There is an ideal apple. There is an ideal tree. There is an ideal human being, and so on. The matter is the material version of the form. The matter is an imitation of the form. Plato believed material things are always temporary and forms are eternal—this idea became the basis of the Platonic philosophy.

Horizontal integration
Horizontal integration means you are moving "horizontally" in your industry by acquiring or merging with competitors with similar product offerings and customers. In contrast, vertical integration occurs

when an organization takes control of one or more stages in the production or distribution of its products.

NSAIDs (nonsteroidal anti-inflammatory drugs)
Medications used to reduce inflammation and the accompanying pain in conditions such as arthritis and other musculoskeletal disorders. Aspirin and ibuprofen are two common examples of these medications.

Weekend warrior
A person who takes part in physically strenuous activity only on the weekend. Weekend warriors usually spend the workweek at a desk. When the weekend comes around, they participate in sports such as golf or tennis or perform household tasks such as gardening or cleaning the gutters. Knee, shoulder, ankle, and lower back injuries are common in weekend warriors.

Chapter 8

Chuck Close (1940–2021)
American painter and photographer known for painting very large portrait heads. In 1988, when Close was forty-eight years old and well known as a portrait painter, he developed a blood clot in his spine that left him a quadriplegic. Many thought his days as a painter were over. Amazingly, he overcame his disabilities, and even though he was paralyzed, he continued his busy career until his death. He painted from a wheelchair with a brush strapped to his hand.

Bottega dell'Opera del Duomo
The sculpture workshop in Florence, Italy, that was founded in 1296 to create the marbles of the Cathedral of Santa Maria del Fiore (the Duomo). This workshop is used today to maintain the many sculptures that are part of the cathedral. Located just behind the cathedral, the

workshop is a short building on a narrow street, Via dello Studio. I have visited this workshop only to find it closed. But a peek through the windowed doors was still inspiring.

Domenico Ghirlandaio (1448–1494)
Early Renaissance painter from the Florentine school noted for his detailed fresco paintings. It was in Ghirlandaio's workshop that a young apprentice named Michelangelo learned the technique of fresco painting, which he later used when painting the Sistine Chapel ceiling.

John Tusa (b. 1936)
British arts administrator, author, and journalist. For over twenty-five years, Tusa has held senior positions in the worlds of art and journalism. He was formerly the managing director of BBC World Service and the Barbican Arts Centre.

Michael Ondaatje (b. 1943)
Sri Lankan–born Canadian poet and writer. Ondaatje is one of Canada's most important novelists and the author of the widely acclaimed *The English Patient* (1992).

Neuroplasticity
Also called brain plasticity. The ability of the brain to rewire itself and function in a different manner—in other words, the brain's ability to change and adapt as a result of new experiences. Examples of neuroplasticity include studying a new language, learning to paint with watercolors, and figuring out your way around a new city. When we physically engage with things, especially with our hands, we generate a great variety of sensory images. Thinking with your hands draws on neuroscience—we create more neural connections. This produces a creativity that mental reasoning alone might not produce.

Samuel van Hoogstraten (1627–1678)
Dutch painter and poet who also wrote extensively on the theory of painting. Van Hoogstraten was a student of Rembrandt.

Ford Motor Company
An American automobile manufacturer that is multinational. It was founded in 1903 by Henry Ford and remains controlled by the Ford family, which owns a minority of the stock but has a majority of the voting rights. But it was not an easy journey for Henry Ford. He used up all the money from his initial investors without producing a car. He then raised another $60,000 and produced a car only to have the company go bankrupt. Later, in the 1920s, sales went through the floor when Henry refused to update the Model T automobile. But Ford, like his friend Thomas Edison, viewed failure as part of his learning curve. He went on to reduce his car assembly time from fourteen hours to ninety minutes, and the rest is history.

Ulysses S. Grant (1822–1885)
The top Union commander at the end of the Civil War and later the eighteenth president of the United States. At West Point, Grant was a poor student, while his future foe, Robert E. Lee, was one of its greatest students. Grant was also a gifted writer and his autobiography is considered one of the best written by a president.

Bob Dylan (b. 1941)
American singer and songwriter. Dylan was awarded the Nobel Prize for Literature in 2016. He became famous in the 1960s for writing simple but powerful songs on war, civil rights, and racism. This was when America was undergoing major social change. Dylan's music evolved from politically charged folk to electrified rock.

Christopher Reeve (1952–2004)

American actor and director who became famous for playing Superman. In 1995, Reeve was thrown from a horse, incurring a spine injury that paralyzed him from the shoulders down. He used a wheelchair and ventilator until his death nine years later. During this time, he helped put a face on spinal injuries.

Marlon Brando (1924–2004)

American actor considered by some to be one of the most influential actors of all time. Many actors, however, did not enjoy working with him. One reason was his refusal to memorize his lines. Another was that he would sometimes refuse to cooperate with a film director.

Ambulatory surgery center (ASC)

A freestanding facility with operating rooms (as opposed to operating rooms within a hospital). Such facilities provide same-day surgical care. Surgeries performed at an ASC do not require hospital admission. ASCs provide cost-effective services in a less stressful environment and are more convenient than most general hospitals. The first ASC in the United States opened in Phoenix in 1970.

Epic

A privately held provider of electronic medical records (EMRs). Epic facilitates the integration and standardization of workflows. It has become the EMR of choice for most of the large hospital health networks in the United States.

Crayola Factory

Some of the most iconic products associated with America are made in other countries. This is not the case for the crayons and other art products manufactured by Crayola. These are all made in Easton, Pennsylvania. The plant makes approximately three billion crayons per year—in four hundred different colors! HCDS provided healthcare to many Crayola employees. Tours of the plant not only opened my eyes to the employee workplace but also gave me an understanding of the production process for Crayola products, which I used to draw and explain a diagnosis to a patient and continue to use in my art practice.

Disruptive innovation

A process or service that starts at the lower end of a market with products that are less expensive and more accessible. These products then move upmarket and threaten to displace established competitors. I learned about disruptive innovation from Clay Christensen and I witnessed it at Bethlehem Steel.

ACKNOWLEDGMENTS

I have always believed a person is as good as the team they have in place. I have been fortunate enough in this life to have wonderful teams—in the OR at my former company; in my studio, Atelier Lucca; and at my regenerative farm. My wife and I couldn't possibly accomplish all we do without our teams. This book is no exception.

That said, everything I do is made possible because I am loved and supported by my wife. Her support, guidance, and assistance were invaluable throughout the many drafts and rewrites of the publication process. I would also like to thank her sister, Rebecca Scott, for her assistance in organizing my notes. Special thanks to Mat Miller and his entire Book Highlight team. Mat introduced me to Matt Holt at BenBella books and both Mat and Matt are responsible for getting this book into readers' hands. I am so grateful for my publisher, Matt, and the entire BenBella team, including my book designer, Jason Arias, and my editors, especially Katie Dickman, who provided insightful and clear feedback. And finally, thank you to Mary Curran Hackett, without whom there would be no book.

BIBLIOGRAPHY

Andreasen, Nancy C. *The Creative Brain: The Science of Genius*. Plume, 2006.

Andretti, Mario and Bob Collins. *What's It Like Out There?* Doubleday, 1994.

Beadle, Phil. *Dancing About Architecture: A Little Book of Creativity*. Edited by Ian Gilbert. Crown House Publishing, 2009.

Beatty, Jack. *The World According to Peter Drucker*. Free Press, 1998.

Cain, Susan. *Quiet: The Power of Introverts in a World That Can't Stop Talking*. Crown Publishers, 2012.

Christensen, Clayton M., James Allworth, and Karen Dillon. *How Will You Measure Your Life?* Harper Business, 2012.

Christensen, Clayton M., Jerome H. Grossman, and Jason Hwang. *The Innovator's Prescription: A Disruptive Solution for Health Care*. McGraw-Hill, 2009.

Christensen, Tanner. *The Creativity Challenge: Design, Experiment, Test, Innovate, Build, Create, Inspire, and Unleash Your Genius*. Adams Media, 2016.

Connelly, Charlie. "Alberto Giacometti and the Moment That Transformed His Art." *The New European* (The New World website). January 10, 2021. https://www.thenewworld.co.uk/brexit-news-the-great-life-of-alberto-giacometti-6875184.

Currey, Mason, ed. *Daily Rituals: How Artists Work*. Knopf, 2013.

Currey, Mason. *Daily Rituals: Women at Work*. Knopf, 2019.

Csikszentmihalyi, Mihaly. *Creativity: The Flow and the Psychology of Discovery and Invention*. Harper Perennial, 1996.

Csikszentmihalyi, Mihaly. *Flow: The Psychology of Optimal Experience*. Harper & Row, 1990.

Duckworth, Angela. *Grit: The Power of Passion and Perseverance*. Scribner, 2016.

Franck, Frederick. *What Matters: Spiritual Nourishment for Mind and Soul*. St. Martin's Press, 1993.

Friedland, Roger and Harold Zellman. *The Fellowship: The Untold Story of Frank Lloyd Wright and the Taliesin Fellowship*. Harper, 2006.

Ghiselin, Brewster, ed. *The Creative Process: A Symposium on Creativity*. University of California Press, 1954.

Gompertz, Will. *Think Like an Artist: and Lead a More Creative, Productive Life*. Viking, 2015.

Hendricks, Gay. *The Big Leap: Conquer Your Hidden Fear and Take Life to the Next Level*. HarperOne, 2009.

Hendricks, Gay. *The Genius Zone: The Breakthrough Process to End Negative Thinking and Live in True Creativity*. St. Martin's Essentials, 2021.

Hourly History. *Pierre-Auguste Renoir: A Life from Beginning to End*. Hourly History, 2020.

Hu, Jing and Jacob B. Hirsh, "Accepting Lower Salaries for Meaningful Work," *Frontiers in Psychology* 8 (2017): Article 1649.

Jackson, Philip W. *John Dewey and the Lessons of Art*. Yale University Press, 1998.

Johansson, Frans. *The Medici Effect: What Elephants and Epidemics Can Teach Us About Innovation*. Harvard Business Review Press, 2004.

Jeffrey, Scott. *Creativity Revealed: Discovering the Source of Inspiration*. Creative Crayon Publishers, 2008.

Kaufman, Scott Barry. *Transcend: The New Science of Self-Actualization*. TarcherPerigee, 2020.

Kaufman, Scott Barry, and Carolyn Gregoire. *Wired to Create: Unraveling the Mysteries of the Creative Mind*. Perigee Books, 2015.

Kazanjian, Dodie and Calvin Tomkins. *Alex: The Life of Alexander Liberman.* Knopf, 1993.

Kimmelman, Michael. "The Complexities of Seeing," review of *The Complexities of Seeing*, by David Sylvester. The New York Times, 1996.

Kissinger, Henry A., Eric Schmidt, and Daniel Huttenlocher. *The Age of AI: And Our Human Future.* Little, Brown, 2021.

Kleinke, J. D. *Oxymorons: The Myth of a U.S. Health Care System.* Jossey-Bass, 2001.

Kleon, Austin. *Keep Going: 10 Ways to Stay Creative in Good Times and Bad.* Workman Publishing, 2019.

Kleon, Austin. *The Steal Like an Artist Journal: A Notebook for Creative Kleptomaniacs.* Workman Publishing, 2015.

Lambert, Kelly. *Lifting Depression: A Neuroscientist's Hands-On Approach to Activating Your Brain's Healing Power.* Basic Books, 2008. Excerpt printed in *Scientific American Mind*, September 2008.

Maslow, A. H. *The Farther Reaches of Human Nature.* Viking Press, 1971.

Nestor, James. *Breath: The New Science of a Lost Art.* Riverhead Books, 2020.

Ondaatje, Michael. *The English Patient.* Vintage International, 1993.

Oppenheimer, Paul. *Rubens: A Portrait.* Cooper Square Press, 2002.

Peters, Tom. *Re-Imagine! Business Excellence in a Disruptive Age.* DK Publishing, 2003.

Pressfield, Steven. *The Artist's Journey: The Wake of the Hero's Journey and the Lifelong Pursuit of Meaning.* Black Irish Entertainment, 2018.

Pressfield, Steven. *Do the Work.* Black Irish Entertainment, 2011.

Pressfield, Steven. *Nobody Wants to Read Your Sh*t: Why That Is and What You Can Do About It.* Black Irish Entertainment, 2016.

Pressfield, Steven. *The War of Art: Break Through the Blocks and Win Your Inner Creative Battles.* Black Irish Entertainment, 2002.

Ratcliffe, Eleanor, Birgitta Gatersleben, Paul T. Sowden, and Kalevi M. Korpela, "Understanding the Perceived Benefits of Nature for Creativity," *Journal of Environmental Psychology* 63 (2019).

Rookmaaker, Hans. *Art Needs No Justification.* InterVarsity Press, 1978.

Saltz, Jerry. *How to Be an Artist.* Riverhead Books, 2020.

Sawyer, R. Keith. *Explaining Creativity: The Science of Human Innovation*. 2nd ed. Oxford University Press, 2012.

Sawyer, R. Keith. *Zig Zag: The Surprising Path to Greater Creativity.* Jossey-Bass, 2013.

Seligman, Isabel. *Lines of Thought: Drawing from Michelangelo to Now.* British Museum Press, 2016.

Senge, Peter, M. *The Fifth Discipline: The Art and Practice of the Learning Organization*. New York: Doubleday, 1990.

Shipley, Lucy. *The Etruscans: Lost Civilizations*. Reaktion Books, 2017.

Smith, Morgan. "70% of Gen Z and Millennials Are Considering Leaving Their Jobs Soon," CNBC, January 18, 2023.

Steinbeck, John. *Steinbeck: A Life in Letters*, ed. Elaine Steinbeck and Robert Wallsten. Penguin, 1989.

Tharp, Twyla. *The Creative Habit: Learn It and Use It for Life.* Simon & Schuster, 2003.

Tharp, Twyla. *Keep It Moving: Lessons for the Rest of Your Life.* Simon & Schuster, 2019.

Wallas, Graham. *The Art of Thought.* Harcourt, Brace, 1926.

Weisberg, Robert W. *Creativity: Beyond the Myth of Genius.* W. H. Freeman, 1993.

Weisberg, Robert W. *Creativity: Genius and Other Myths.* W. H. Freeman, 1986.

White, Michael. *Leonardo: The First Scientist.* St. Martin's Press, 2000.

ABOUT THE AUTHOR

Emilio DiIorio is a sculptor and painter. As a former systems engineer, orthopedic surgeon, and CEO, he has studied the science and art of creativity throughout his career. He has a degree in engineering from New York University and studied economics at NYU's Stern School of Business. In Europe, he studied anatomy at Ghent University before deciding to enroll at medical school at the University of Antwerp. He completed clinical medical studies and a residency in orthopedic surgery at Boston University and the Lahey Clinic. He is a fellow of the American Academy of Orthopedic Surgeons. Dr. DiIorio founded and was CEO of an innovative regional healthcare delivery network in northeastern Pennsylvania and western New Jersey. He sold the company in 2019 and continued the practice and study of sculpture, the fine arts, and the creative process, which he pursued for decades while serving as an orthopedic surgeon and entrepreneur. Of late, he has also begun to study and put into practice regenerative organic farming. He currently works with his creative team at Atelier Lucca—sculpture and painting studios, gardens, and a private art gallery in Bethlehem, Pennsylvania. He divides his time between Bethlehem, a working farm in the Pocono Mountains, and a home in Manhattan.